New Perspectives on

MICROSOFT
WINDOWS XP

Brief

JUNE JAMRICH PARSONS

DAN OJA

JOAN & PATRICK CAREY
Carey Associates

LISA RUFFOLO

COURSE
TECHNOLOGY

THOMSON LEARNING ™

Australia • Canada • Mexico • Singapore • Spain • United Kingdom • United States

**COURSE
TECHNOLOGY**

™

THOMSON LEARNING

New Perspectives on Microsoft® Windows XP—Brief

is published by Course Technology.

Managing Editor:
Greg Donald

Senior Editor:
Donna Gridley

Senior Product Manager:
Kathy Finnegan

Product Manager:
Melissa Hathaway

Technology Product Manager:
Amanda Young

Editorial Assistant:
Jessica Engstrom

Marketing Manager:
Sean Teare

Developmental Editor:
Kim Crowley

Production Editor:
Kristen Guevara

Composition:
GEX Publishing Services

Text Designer:
Meral Dabcovich

Cover Designer:
Efrat Reis

Preface

Course Technology is the world leader in information technology education. The New Pers
Series is an integral part of Course Technology's success. Visit our Web site to see a whole
perspective on teaching and learning solutions.

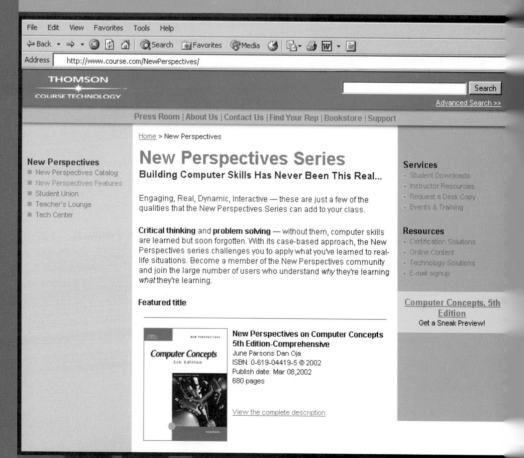

File   Edit   View   Favorites   Tools   Help

⇐ Back ▾ ⇒ ▾ ⊗ ⟳ ⌂ | Search   Favorites   Media ⟳ | ⟱▾ ⟳ W ▾ ⟳

Address | http://www.course.com/NewPerspectives/

THOMSON

COURSE TECHNOLOGY

Search

Advanced Search >>

Press Room | About Us | Contact Us | Find Your Rep | Bookstore | Support

Home > New Perspectives

New Perspectives
- New Perspectives Catalog
- New Perspectives Features
- Student Union
- Teacher's Lounge
- Tech Center

New Perspectives Series
Building Computer Skills Has Never Been This Real...

Engaging, Real, Dynamic, Interactive — these are just a few of the
qualities that the New Perspectives Series can add to your class.

Critical thinking and **problem solving** — without them, computer skills
are learned but soon forgotten. With its case-based approach, the New
Perspectives series challenges you to apply what you've learned to real-
life situations. Become a member of the New Perspectives community
and join the large number of users who understand *why* they're learning
what they're learning.

Featured title

**New Perspectives on Computer Concepts
5th Edition-Comprehensive**
June Parsons Dan Oja
ISBN: 0-619-04419-5 © 2002
Publish date: Mar 08,2002
680 pages

View the complete description

Services
- Student Downloads
- Instructor Resources
- Request a Desk Copy
- Events & Training

Resources
- Certification Solutions
- Online Content
- Technology Solutions
- E-mail signup

**Computer Concepts, 5th
Edition**
Get a Sneak Preview!

New Perspectives—Building Computer Skills Has Never Been This

Why New Perspectives will work for you.

Critical thinking and **problem solving**—without them, computer skills are learned but soon forgotten. With its **case-based** approach, the New Perspectives Series challenges students to apply what they've learned to real-life situations. Become a member of the New Perspectives community and watch your students not only **master** computer skills, but also **retain** and carry this **knowledge** into the world.

New Perspectives catalog
Our online catalog is never out of date! Go to the Catalog link on our Web site to check out our available titles, request a desk copy, download a book preview, or locate online files.

Complete system of offerings
Whether you're looking for a Brief book, an Advanced book, or something in between, we've got you covered. Go to the Catalog link on our Web site to find the level of coverage that's right for you.

Instructor materials
We have all the tools you need—data files, solution files, figure files, a sample syllabus, and ExamView, our powerful testing software package.

How well do your students know Microsoft Office?
Experience the power, ease, and flexibility of SAM XP and TOM. These innovative software tools provide the first truly integrated technology-based training and assessment solution for your applications course. Click the Tech Center link to learn more.

Get certified
If you want to get certified, we have the titles for you. Find out more by clicking the Teacher's Lounge link.

Interested in online learning?
Enhance your course with rich online content for use through MyCourse 2.0, WebCT, and Blackboard. Go to the Teacher's Lounge to find the platform that's right for you.

**Your link to the future is at
www.course.com/NewPerspectives**

What you need to know about this book.

- Student Online Companion takes students to the Web for additional work.

- ExamView testing software gives you the option of generating a printed test, LAN-based test, or test over the Internet.

- New Perspectives Labs provide students with self-paced practice on computer-related topics.

- The step-by-step instructions and screen illustrations guide students as they tour the Windows XP desktop, practice using the mouse, and explore Windows XP online Help.

- Students will appreciate the contemporary, realistic scenarios that place them in the context of a computer lab and a distance learning course.

- This text provides a comprehensive overview of working with Windows XP. It moves quickly and is suitable for both beginning students and experienced students, who can use it as a review.

CASE	TROUBLE?	SESSION 1.1	QUICK CHECK	RW
Tutorial Case Each tutorial begins with a problem presented in a case that is meaningful to students. The case sets the scene to help students understand what they will do in the tutorial.	**TROUBLE? Paragraphs** These paragraphs anticipate the mistakes or problems that students may have and help them continue with the tutorial.	**Sessions** Each tutorial is divided into sessions designed to be completed in about 45 minutes each. Students should take as much time as they need and take a break between sessions.	**Quick Check Questions** Each session concludes with conceptual Quick Check questions that test students' understanding of what they learned in the session.	**Reference Windows** Reference Windows are succinct summaries of the most important tasks covered in a tutorial. They preview actions students will perform in the steps to follow.

TABLE OF CONTENTS

Acknowledgments

Many thanks to everyone on the New Perspectives team for their guidance, insight, and good humor, including Greg Donald, Jessica Engstrom, and Kristen Guevara. Special thanks to Kathy Finnegan, whose common sense and dedication to the reader informs this book, and Kim Crowley, who approached each draft with freshness and improved the book with every edit. I also appreciate the careful work of Harris Bierhoff, Quality Assurance tester, and Risa Blair, Hilda Wirth Federico, and Eric Johnston, who reviewed these tutorials. Special thanks to June Parsons, Dan Oja, and Joan and Patrick Carey, on whose previous work this book is based.

—Lisa Ruffolo

New Perspectives on

MICROSOFT®
WINDOWS XP

Read This Before You Begin

To the Student

Data Disks

To complete the Level I tutorials, Review Assignments, and Projects, you need three Data Disks. Your instructor will either provide you with the Data Disks or ask you to make your own.

If you are making your own Data Disks, you will need **three** blank, formatted high-density disks. You will need to copy a set of files and/or folders from a file server, standalone computer, or the Web onto your disks. Your instructor will tell you which computer, drive letter, and folders contain the files you need. You could also download the files by going to www.course.com and following the instructions on the screen.

The information below shows you the Data Disks you need so that you will have enough disk space to complete all the tutorials, Review Assignments, and Projects:

Data Disk 1

Write this on the disk label:
Windows XP Tutorial 2 Data Disk

Data Disk 2

Write this on the disk label:
Windows XP Disk 1 Data Disk Copy

Data Disk 3

Write this on the disk label:
Windows XP Tutorial 2, Assignment 4

When you begin each tutorial, Review Assignment, or Project, be sure you are using the correct Data Disk. Refer to the "File Finder" chart at the back of this text for more detailed information on which files are used in which tutorials. See the inside front or inside back cover of this book for more information on Data Disk files, or ask your instructor or technical support person for assistance.

Course Labs

The Windows XP Level I tutorials feature three interactive Course Labs to help you understand how to use a keyboard and a mouse, and how to work with files. There are Lab Assignments at the end of Tutorial 1 and Tutorial 2 that relate to these Labs.

To start a Lab, click the **Start** button on the Windows taskbar, point to **Programs**, point to **Course Labs**, point to **New Perspectives Course Labs**, and then click the name of the Lab you want to use.

Using Your Own Computer

If you are going to work through this book using your own computer, you need:

- **Computer System** Microsoft Windows XP must be installed on your computer. This book assumes a typical installation of Microsoft Windows XP Professional.

- **Data Disks** You will not be able to complete the tutorials or exercises in this book using your own computer until you have your Data Disks.

- **Course Labs** See your instructor or technical support person to obtain the Course Lab software for use on your own computer.

Visit Our World Wide Web Site

Additional materials designed especially for you are available on the World Wide Web.
Go to www.course.com/NewPerspectives.

To the Instructor

The Data Disk Files and Course Labs are available on the Instructor's Resource Kit for this title. Follow the instructions in the Help file on the CD-ROM to install the programs to your network or standalone computer. For information on creating Data Disks or the Course Labs, see the "To the Student" section above.

You are granted a license to copy the Data Files and Course Labs to any computer or computer network used by students who have purchased this book.

In this tutorial you will:

- Start and shut down Windows XP

- Identify the objects on the Windows XP desktop

- Practice mouse functions

- Run software programs, switch between them, and close them

- Identify and use the controls in a window

- Use Windows XP controls, such as menus, toolbars, list boxes, scroll bars, option buttons, tabs, and check boxes

- Explore Windows XP Help

Using a Keyboard   Using a Mouse

EXPLORING THE BASICS

Investigating the Windows XP Operating System

CASE

Your First Day at the Computer

You walk into the computer lab and sit down at a desk. There are computers in front of you, and you find yourself staring dubiously at the screen. Where to start? As if in answer to your question, your friend Steve Laslow appears.

"You start with the operating system," says Steve. Noticing your puzzled look, Steve explains that the **operating system** is software that helps the computer carry out operating tasks, such as displaying information on the computer screen and saving data on disks. (Software refers to the **programs**, or **applications**, that a computer uses to perform tasks.) Your computer uses the **Microsoft Windows XP** operating system—**Windows XP** for short.

Steve explains that much of the software created for use with Windows XP shares the same look and works the same way. This similarity in design means that once you have learned to use one Windows program, such as Microsoft Word (a word-processing program), you are well on your way to understanding how to use other Windows programs. Windows XP allows you to use more than one program at a time, so you can easily switch between your word-processing program and your address book program, for example. Windows XP also makes it very easy to access the **Internet**, the worldwide collection of computers connected to one another to enable communication. All in all, Windows XP makes your computer an effective and easy-to-use productivity tool.

In this tutorial you will start Microsoft Windows XP and practice some basic computer skills.

SESSION 1.1

In this session, you will learn some basic Windows terminology. You will use a pointing device, start and close a program, and switch between programs that are running at the same time.

Starting Windows XP

Using a Keyboard

Windows XP automatically starts when you turn on your computer. Depending on the way your computer is set up, you might be asked to enter your username and password.

To start Windows XP:

1. Turn on your computer. After a moment, Windows XP starts and displays the Windows XP Welcome screen.

TROUBLE? If you are asked to select an operating system, do not take action. Windows XP should start automatically after a designated number of seconds. If it does not, ask your instructor or technical support person for help.

TROUBLE? If this is the first time you have started your computer with Windows XP, messages might appear on your screen informing you that Windows is setting up components of your computer. Wait until the Welcome screen appears, and then continue with Step 2.

2. On the Welcome screen, click your user name. The Windows XP screen appears, as shown in Figure 1-1.

TROUBLE? If your user name does not appear on the Welcome screen, ask your instructor which name you should click.

TROUBLE? If prompted to do so, type your assigned user name, press the Tab key, type your password, and then click OK or press the Enter key to continue.

Figure 1-1	THE WINDOWS XP DESKTOP

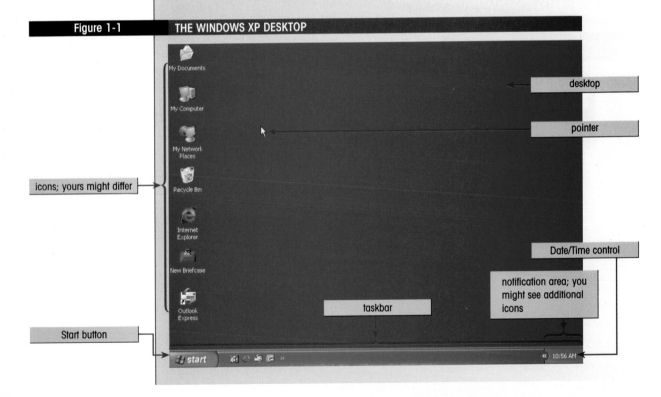

3. Look at your screen and locate the objects labeled in Figure 1-1. The objects on your screen might appear larger or smaller than those in Figure 1-1, depending on your monitor's settings. Figure 1-2 describes the function of each of these objects.

Figure 1-2	ELEMENTS OF THE WINDOWS XP DESKTOP

ELEMENT	DESCRIPTION
Icon	A small picture that represents an object available to your computer
Pointer	A small object, such as an arrow, that moves on the screen when you move the mouse
Desktop	Your workplace on the screen
Date/Time control	Shows the current date and time and lets you set the clock
Taskbar	Contains buttons that give you quick access to common tools and the programs currently running
Start button	Provides access to Windows XP programs, documents, and information on the Internet
Notification area	Displays icons corresponding to services running in the background, such as an Internet connection

TROUBLE? One default setting for your computer might be to use a screen saver, a program that causes the monitor to go blank or to display an animated design after a specified amount of idle time. If a blank screen or animated design replaces the Window XP desktop, you can press any key or move the mouse to restore the Windows XP desktop.

The Windows XP desktop uses a **graphical user interface** (**GUI**, pronounced "gooey"), which displays **icons**, or pictures of familiar objects, such as file folders and documents, to represent items stored on your computer, such as programs and files. Windows XP gets its name from the rectangular work areas, called "windows," that appear on your screen as you work. No windows should be open right now. You will learn more about windows in Session 1.2.

The Windows XP Desktop

In Windows terminology, the area that appears on your screen when Windows XP starts represents a **desktop**—a workspace for projects and the tools that you need to manipulate your projects. When you first start a computer, it uses **default settings**, those preset by the operating system. The default desktop you see after you first install Windows XP, for example, might have a plain blue background. However, Microsoft designed Windows XP so that you can easily change the appearance of the desktop. You can, for example, change color, or add patterns, images, and text to the desktop background.

Many organizations design customized desktops for their computers. Figure 1-1 shows the default Windows XP desktop. Figure 1-3 shows two other examples of desktops, one designed for a business, North Pole Novelties, and one designed for a school, the University of Colorado. Although your desktop might not look exactly like any of the examples in Figure 1-1 or Figure 1-3, you should be able to locate similar objects on your screen.

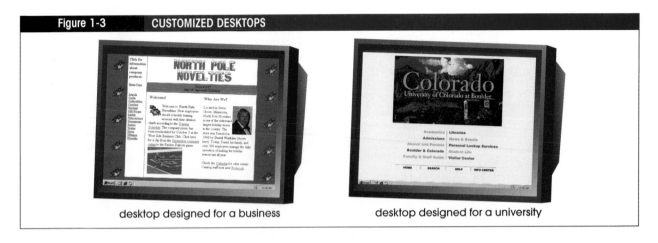

Figure 1-3	CUSTOMIZED DESKTOPS

desktop designed for a business   desktop designed for a university

Using a Pointing Device

Using a Mouse

A **pointing device** helps you interact with objects on your computer screen. Pointing devices come in many shapes and sizes; some are designed to ensure that your hand won't tire while using them. Some attach directly to your computer via a cable, whereas others function like a TV remote control and allow you to access your computer without being right next to it. Figure 1-4 shows examples of common pointing devices.

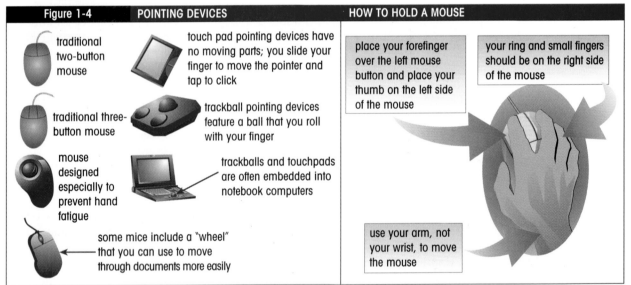

Figure 1-4	POINTING DEVICES	HOW TO HOLD A MOUSE

traditional two-button mouse

touch pad pointing devices have no moving parts; you slide your finger to move the pointer and tap to click

place your forefinger over the left mouse button and place your thumb on the left side of the mouse

your ring and small fingers should be on the right side of the mouse

traditional three-button mouse

trackball pointing devices feature a ball that you roll with your finger

mouse designed especially to prevent hand fatigue

trackballs and touchpads are often embedded into notebook computers

some mice include a "wheel" that you can use to move through documents more easily

use your arm, not your wrist, to move the mouse

The most common pointing device is called a **mouse**, so this book uses that term. If you are using a different pointing device, such as a trackball, substitute that device whenever you see the term *mouse*. Because Windows XP uses a GUI, you need to know how to use the mouse to manipulate the objects on the screen. In this session, you will learn about pointing and clicking. In Session 1.2, you will learn how to use the mouse to move objects.

You can also interact with objects by using the keyboard; however, the mouse is more convenient for most tasks, so the tutorials in this book assume that you are using one.

Pointing

You use a pointing device to move the mouse pointer over objects on the desktop. The pointer is usually shaped like an arrow ⍔, although the pointer will change shape depending on its location and on the tasks you are performing. Most computer users place the mouse on a **mouse pad**, a flat piece of rubber that helps the mouse move smoothly. As you move the mouse on the mouse pad, the pointer on the screen moves in a corresponding direction.

You begin most Windows operations by positioning the pointer over a specific part of the screen. This is called **pointing**.

To move the pointer:

1. Position your right index finger over the left mouse button, as shown in Figure 1-4, but don't click yet. Lightly grasp the sides of the mouse with your thumb and little finger.

TROUBLE? If you want to use the mouse with your left hand, ask your instructor or technical support person to help you use the Control Panel to swap the functions of the left and right mouse buttons. Be sure to find out how to change back to the right-handed mouse setting, so that you can reset the mouse each time you are finished in the lab.

2. Place the mouse on the mouse pad, and then move the mouse. Watch the movement of the pointer.

TROUBLE? If you run out of room to move your mouse, lift the mouse and place it in the middle of the mouse pad. Notice that the pointer does not move when the mouse is not in contact with the mouse pad or another surface.

When you position the mouse pointer over certain objects, such as the objects on the taskbar, tips appear. These tips are called **ScreenTips**, and tell you the purpose or function of the object to which you are pointing.

To view ScreenTips:

1. Use the mouse to point to the **Start** button ⊞ start on the taskbar. After a few seconds, you see the ScreenTip "Click here to begin," as shown in Figure 1-5.

Figure 1-5	VIEWING SCREENTIPS

ScreenTip

pointer

2. Point to the time displayed in the notification area at the right end of the taskbar. Notice that a ScreenTip for today's date (or the date to which your computer's time clock is set) appears.

Clicking

Clicking refers to pressing a mouse button and immediately releasing it. Clicking sends a signal to your computer that you want to perform an action on the object you click. In Windows XP you perform most actions with the left mouse button. If you are told to click an object, position the mouse pointer on it and click the left mouse button, unless instructed otherwise.

When you click the Start button, the Start menu opens. A **menu** is a list of options that you can use to complete tasks. The **Start menu** provides you with access to programs, documents, and much more. Try clicking the Start button to open the Start menu.

To open the Start menu:

1. Point to the **Start** button [start] on the taskbar.

2. Click the left mouse button. The Start menu opens. Notice the arrow ▶ following the All Programs option on the Start menu. This arrow indicates that you can view additional choices by navigating to a **submenu**, a menu extending from the main menu. See Figure 1-6.

Figure 1-6	START MENU

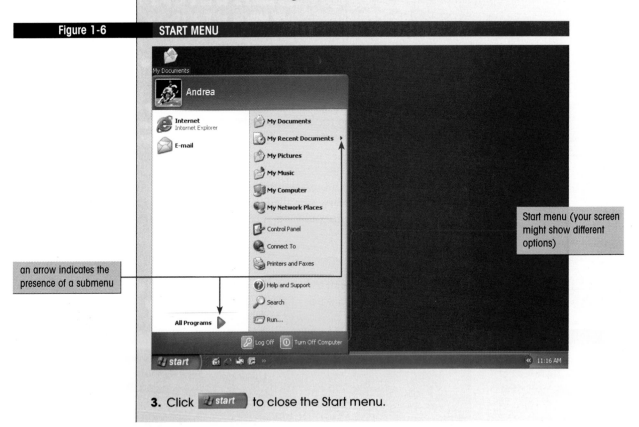

an arrow indicates the presence of a submenu

Start menu (your screen might show different options)

3. Click [start] to close the Start menu.

Next you'll learn how to select items on a submenu.

Selecting

In Windows XP, you point to and then click an object to **select** it. You need to select an object to work with it. Windows XP shows you which object is selected by highlighting it, usually by changing the object's color, putting a box around it, or making the object appear to be pushed in, as shown in Figure 1-7.

Figure 1-7	SELECTED OBJECTS

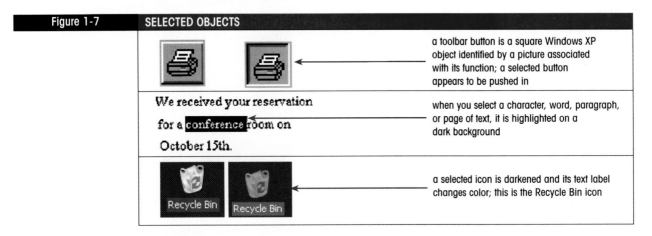

a toolbar button is a square Windows XP object identified by a picture associated with its function; a selected button appears to be pushed in

We received your reservation for a conference room on October 15th.

when you select a character, word, paragraph, or page of text, it is highlighted on a dark background

a selected icon is darkened and its text label changes color; this is the Recycle Bin icon

In Windows XP, depending on your computer's settings, you can select certain objects by pointing to them and others by clicking them. Try pointing to the All Programs option on the Start menu to open the All Programs submenu.

To select an option on a menu:

1. Click the **Start** button 🐾 *start* on the taskbar, and notice how it appears to be pushed in, indicating that it is selected.

2. Point to (but don't click) **All Programs** on the Start menu. When you first point to the All Programs option, it is highlighted to indicate it is selected. After a short pause, the All Programs submenu opens. See Figure 1-8.

   TROUBLE? If a submenu other than the All Programs menu opens, you pointed to the wrong option. Move the mouse so that the pointer points to All Programs.

| Figure 1-8 | ALL PROGRAMS SUBMENU |

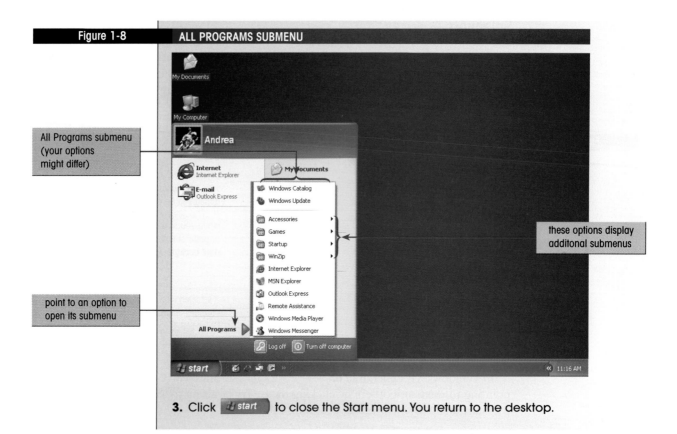

All Programs submenu (your options might differ)

these options display additonal submenus

point to an option to open its submenu

3. Click ⊞start to close the Start menu. You return to the desktop.

Double-Clicking

In addition to clicking an object to select it, you can double-click an object to open or start the item associated to it. For example, you can double-click a folder icon to open the folder and see its contents. Or you can double-click a program icon to start the program. Double-clicking means to click the mouse button twice in quick succession.

You can practice double-clicking now by opening the My Documents folder. **My Documents** is your personal folder, a convenient place to store documents, graphics, and other work.

To open the My Documents folder:

1. Click and then point to the **My Documents** icon on the desktop. After a few moments, a ScreenTip appears describing the My Documents folder.

TROUBLE? If you don't see the icons for My Computer or My Documents, you can add them to the desktop. Click Start, click Control Panel, click Switch to Category New, if necessary, click Appearance and Themes, and then click Change the desktop background. In the Desktop Items dialog box, click to insert checks in the boxes for My Computer and My Documents to add these icons to the desktop. You can also add icons for My Network Places and Internet Explorer. Click OK to close each dialog box.

2. Click the left mouse button twice quickly to double-click the **My Documents** icon. The My Documents window opens, as shown in Figure 1-9.

Figure 1-9	CONTENTS OF THE MY DOCUMENTS FOLDER

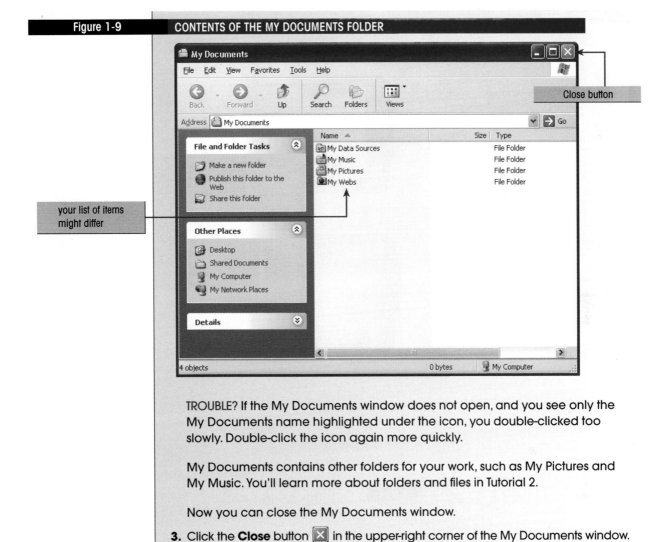

TROUBLE? If the My Documents window does not open, and you see only the My Documents name highlighted under the icon, you double-clicked too slowly. Double-click the icon again more quickly.

My Documents contains other folders for your work, such as My Pictures and My Music. You'll learn more about folders and files in Tutorial 2.

Now you can close the My Documents window.

3. Click the **Close** button ⊠ in the upper-right corner of the My Documents window.

You'll learn more about opening and closing windows in Session 1.2.

Right-Clicking

Pointing devices were originally designed with a single button, so the term "clicking" had only one meaning: you pressed that button. Innovations in technology, however, led to the addition of a second and even a third button (and more recently, options such as a wheel) that expanded the pointing device's capabilities. More recent programs—especially those designed for Windows XP—take advantage of additional buttons, especially the right button. However, the term "clicking" continues to refer to the left button; clicking an object with the *right* button is called **right-clicking**.

In Windows XP, right-clicking both selects an object and opens its **shortcut menu**, which is a list of options directly related to the object that you right-clicked. You can right-click practically any object—the Start button, a desktop icon, the taskbar, and even the desktop itself—to view options associated with that object. For example, the illustration in the top portion of Figure 1-10 shows what happens when you click the Start button with the left mouse button to open the Start menu. Clicking the Start button with the right button, however, opens the Start button's shortcut menu, as shown in the second illustration.

Figure 1-10   **CLICKING WITH THE LEFT AND RIGHT MOUSE BUTTONS**

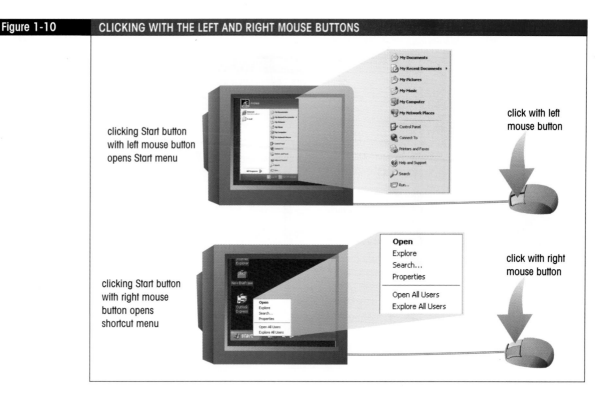

clicking Start button
with left mouse button
opens Start menu

click with left
mouse button

clicking Start button
with right mouse
button opens
shortcut menu

| Open |
| Explore |
| Search... |
| Properties |
| Open All Users |
| Explore All Users |

click with right
mouse button

Try right-clicking to open the shortcut menu for the Start button.

To right-click an object:

1. Position the pointer over the Start button  on the taskbar.

2. Right-click  to open the Start button's shortcut menu. This menu offers a list of options available to the Start menu.

TROUBLE? If you are using a trackball or a mouse with three buttons or a wheel, make sure you click the button on the far right, not the one in the middle.

TROUBLE? Your menu may look slightly different from the one in Figure 1-11. Different computers often have different options and commands.

Figure 1-11   **START BUTTON SHORTCUT MENU**

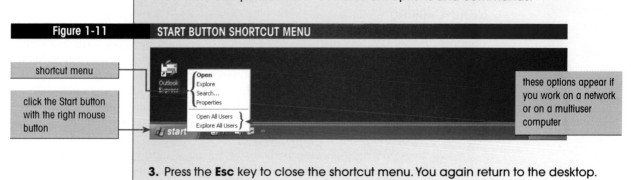

shortcut menu

click the Start button
with the right mouse
button

these options appear if
you work on a network
or on a multiuser
computer

3. Press the **Esc** key to close the shortcut menu. You again return to the desktop.

Starting and Closing a Program

To use a program, such as a word-processing program, you must first start it. With Windows XP you start a program by clicking the Start button and then locating and clicking the program's name in the submenus.

The Reference Window below explains how to start a program. Don't do the steps in the Reference Window now; they are for your reference later.

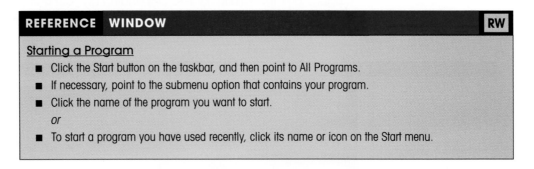

REFERENCE WINDOW **RW**

Starting a Program
- Click the Start button on the taskbar, and then point to All Programs.
- If necessary, point to the submenu option that contains your program.
- Click the name of the program you want to start.
  or
- To start a program you have used recently, click its name or icon on the Start menu.

Windows XP includes an easy-to-use word-processing program called WordPad. Suppose you want to start the WordPad program and use it to write a letter or report. You open Windows XP programs from the Start menu. Programs are usually located on the All Programs submenu or on one of its submenus. To start WordPad, for example, you navigate to the All Programs and Accessories submenus.

To start the WordPad program from the Start menu:

1. Click the **Start** button ⊎ start on the taskbar to open the Start menu.

2. Point to **All Programs** to display the All Programs submenu.

3. Point to **Accessories**. Another submenu opens. Figure 1-12 shows the open menus.

Figure 1-12   **START MENU AND RELATED SUBMENUS**

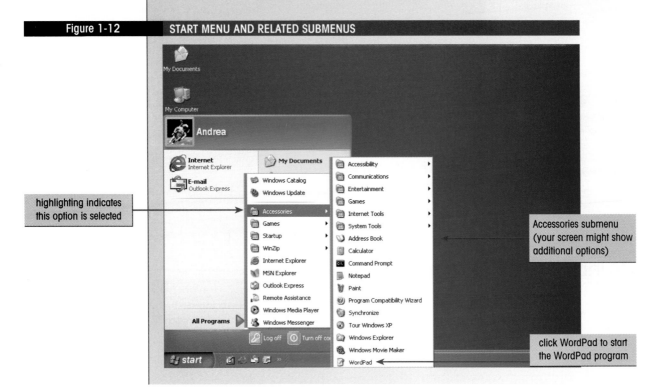

highlighting indicates this option is selected

Accessories submenu (your screen might show additional options)

click WordPad to start the WordPad program

TROUBLE? If a different menu opens, you might have moved the mouse too slowly so that a different submenu opened. Move the pointer back to the All Programs option, and then move the pointer up or down to point to Accessories. Once you're more comfortable moving the mouse, you'll find that you can eliminate this problem by moving the mouse quickly.

4. Click **WordPad** on the Accessories submenu. The WordPad program window opens, as shown in Figure 1-13. Depending on your computer settings, the WordPad program window may fill the entire screen. You will learn how to manipulate windows in Session 1.2.

| Figure 1-13 | THE WORDPAD PROGRAM WINDOW |

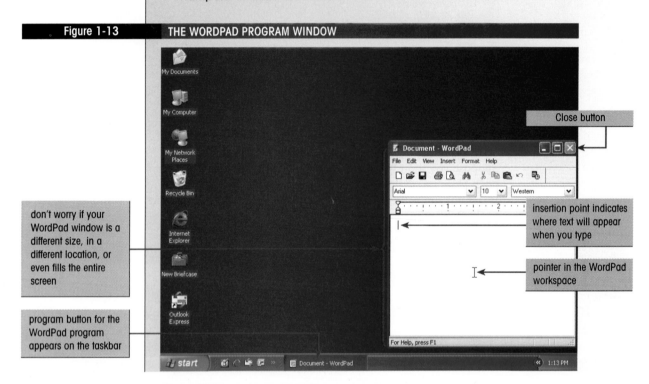

don't worry if your WordPad window is a different size, in a different location, or even fills the entire screen

program button for the WordPad program appears on the taskbar

Close button

insertion point indicates where text will appear when you type

pointer in the WordPad workspace

When you start a program, it is said to be **open** or **running**. A **program button** appears on the taskbar for each open program. You click a program button to switch between open programs. When you finish using a program, you can click the Close button located in the upper-right corner of the program window.

To exit the WordPad program:

1. Click the **Close** button ☒ on the WordPad title bar. You return to the Windows XP desktop.

Running **Multiple Programs**

One of the most useful features of Windows XP is its ability to run multiple programs at the same time. This feature, known as **multitasking**, allows you to work on more than one project at a time and switch quickly between projects. For example, you can start WordPad and leave it running while you then start the Paint program.

To run WordPad and Paint at the same time:

1. Start WordPad again and then click the **Start** button start .

2. Point to **All Programs** and then point to **Accessories**.

3. Click **Paint**. The Paint program window opens, as shown in Figure 1-14. Now two programs are running at the same time.

Figure 1-14	THE PAINT PROGRAM

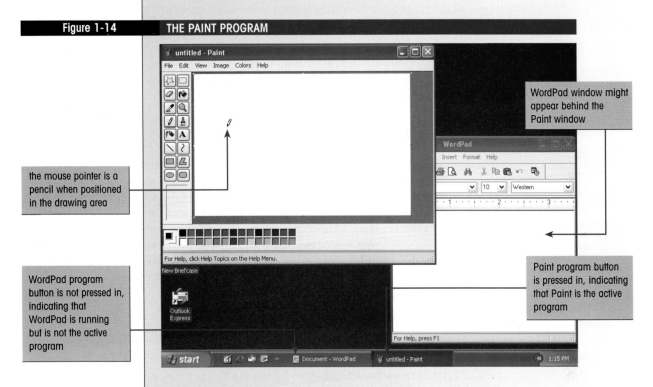

the mouse pointer is a pencil when positioned in the drawing area

WordPad window might appear behind the Paint window

WordPad program button is not pressed in, indicating that WordPad is running but is not the active program

Paint program button is pressed in, indicating that Paint is the active program

TROUBLE? The Paint program may fill the entire screen. You will learn how to manipulate windows in Session 1.2.

What happened to WordPad? The WordPad program button is still on the taskbar, indicating that WordPad is still running even if you cannot see its program window. Try to imagine that the WordPad program window is stacked behind the Paint program window, as illustrated in Figure 1-15. Paint is the active program because it is the one with which you are currently working.

Figure 1-15	PROJECTS STACKED ON A DESK

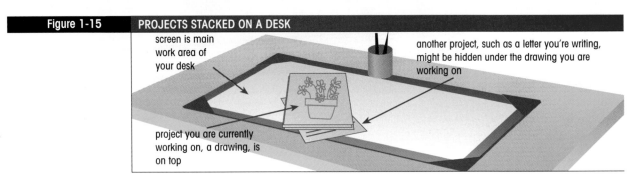

screen is main work area of your desk

another project, such as a letter you're writing, might be hidden under the drawing you are working on

project you are currently working on, a drawing, is on top

Switching Between Programs

The easiest way to switch between programs is to use the program buttons on the taskbar.

To switch between WordPad and Paint:

1. Click the program button labeled **Document - WordPad** on the taskbar. The WordPad program window moves to the front, and now the Document - WordPad button looks as if it has been pushed in, indicating that it is the active program.

2. Click the program button labeled **untitled - Paint** on the taskbar to switch to the Paint program. The Paint program is again the active program.

Using the Quick Launch Toolbar

The Windows XP taskbar displays buttons for programs currently running. The taskbar also can contain **toolbars**, sets of buttons that give single-click access to programs or documents that aren't running or open. For example, the Windows XP taskbar can display the **Quick Launch toolbar**, which gives quick access to Internet programs and to the desktop. Your taskbar might contain additional toolbars or none at all.

When you are running more than one program but you want to return to the desktop, perhaps to use one of the desktop icons, such as My Computer, you can do so by using one of the Quick Launch toolbar buttons. Clicking the Show Desktop button returns you to the desktop. The open programs are not closed; they are simply inactive and reduced to buttons on the taskbar.

To return to the desktop:

1. Click the **Show Desktop** button 🗖 on the Quick Launch toolbar. The desktop displays, and both the Paint and WordPad programs are temporarily inactive. See Figure 1-16.

   TROUBLE? If the Quick Launch toolbar is not visible on your taskbar, right-click the taskbar, point to Toolbars, and then click Quick Launch. Then try Step 1 again.

Figure 1-16	ACCESSING THE DESKTOP

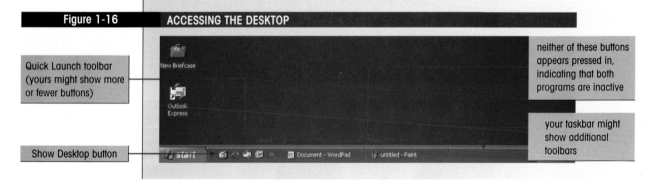

Quick Launch toolbar (yours might show more or fewer buttons)

Show Desktop button

neither of these buttons appears pressed in, indicating that both programs are inactive

your taskbar might show additional toolbars

Closing Inactive Programs from the Taskbar

You should always close a program when you finish using it. Each program uses computer resources, such as memory, so Windows XP works more efficiently when only the programs you need are open. You've already seen how to close an open program using the Close button on the title bar of the program window. You can also close a program, whether active or inactive, by using the shortcut menu associated with the program button on the taskbar.

To close WordPad and Paint using the program button shortcut menus:

1. Right-click the **untitled – Paint** button on the taskbar. Remember that to right-click something, you click it with the right mouse button. The shortcut menu for the Paint program button opens. See Figure 1-17.

Figure 1-17	PROGRAM BUTTON SHORTCUT MENU

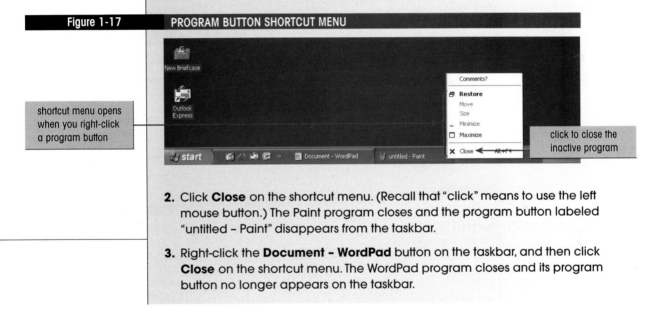

shortcut menu opens when you right-click a program button

click to close the inactive program

2. Click **Close** on the shortcut menu. (Recall that "click" means to use the left mouse button.) The Paint program closes and the program button labeled "untitled – Paint" disappears from the taskbar.

3. Right-click the **Document – WordPad** button on the taskbar, and then click **Close** on the shortcut menu. The WordPad program closes and its program button no longer appears on the taskbar.

Shutting Down Windows XP

You should always shut down Windows XP before you turn off your computer. If you turn off your computer without shutting it down correctly, you might lose data and damage your files.

Typically you will use the Turn Off Computer option on the Start menu when you want to turn off your computer. However, your school might prefer that you select the Log Off option on the Start menu. This option logs you off of Windows XP but leaves the computer on, allowing another user to log on without restarting the computer. Check with your instructor or technical support person for the preferred method at your lab.

To shut down Windows XP:

1. Click the **Start** button ⟪start⟫ on the taskbar.

2. Click **Turn Off Computer**, located at the bottom of the menu. The Turn Off Computer dialog box opens. See Figure 1-18.

TROUBLE? If you are supposed to log off rather than shut down, click Log Off instead and follow your school's logoff procedure.

| Figure 1-18 | SHUTTING DOWN THE COMPUTER |

click to shut down Windows

Turn Off Computer

Stand By   Turn Off   Restart

Cancel

3. Click the **Turn Off** button.

4. Wait until you see a message indicating that it is safe to turn off your computer. If your lab procedure includes switching off your computer after shutting it down, do so now; otherwise leave the computer running. Some computers turn themselves off automatically.

In this session, you have started Windows XP, become familiar with the desktop, and learned how to use the mouse to select menu items. In the next session, you will learn how to work with windows.

Session 1.1 QUICK CHECK

1. What is the purpose of the taskbar?

2. The _____ feature of Windows XP allows you to run more than one program at a time.

3. The _____ is a list of options that provides you with access to programs, documents, submenus, and more.

4. What should you do if you are trying to move the pointer to the left edge of your screen, but your mouse bumps into the keyboard?

5. Even if you cannot see an open program on your desktop, the program might be running. How can you tell if a program is running?

6. Why should you close each program when you finish using it?

7. Why should you shut down Windows XP before you turn off your computer?

SESSION 1.2

In this session you will manipulate windows using controls that are available in Windows XP. You will move a window, and you will also change the size and shape of a window. You will use program menus, toolbars, and controls, such as list boxes and scroll bars, available in windows and dialog boxes. Also in this session, you will use Windows XP Help to gain access to program-related information and tasks.

Anatomy of a Window

Recall from Session 1.1 that when you run a program in Windows XP, the program appears in a window. A **window** is a rectangular area of the screen that contains a program, text, graphics, or data. "Windows," spelled with an uppercase "W," is the name of the Microsoft operating system. The word "window" with a lowercase "w" refers to one of the rectangular areas on the screen. A window also contains **controls**, which are graphical or textual objects used for manipulating the window and for using the program. Figure 1-19 describes the controls you are likely to see in most windows.

Figure 1-19	WINDOW CONTROLS
CONTROL	**DESCRIPTION**
Menu bar	Contains the titles of menus, such as File, Edit, and Help
Sizing buttons	Let you enlarge, shrink, or close a window
Status bar	Provides you with messages relevant to the task you are performing
Title bar	Contains the window title and basic window control buttons
Toolbar	Contains buttons that provide you with shortcuts to common menu commands
Window title	Identifies the program and document contained in the window
Workspace	Part of the window you use to enter your work—to enter text, draw pictures, set up calculations, and so on

The WordPad program is a good example of a typical window. Start WordPad and identify its window controls.

To look at the window controls in WordPad:

1. Make sure that Windows XP is running and the Windows XP desktop is displayed.

2. Start WordPad.

   TROUBLE? To start WordPad, click the Start button, point to All Programs, point to Accessories, and then click WordPad.

3. On your screen, identify the controls that are labeled in Figure 1-20. Your WordPad program window may fill the entire screen or differ in size. You'll learn to change window size shortly.

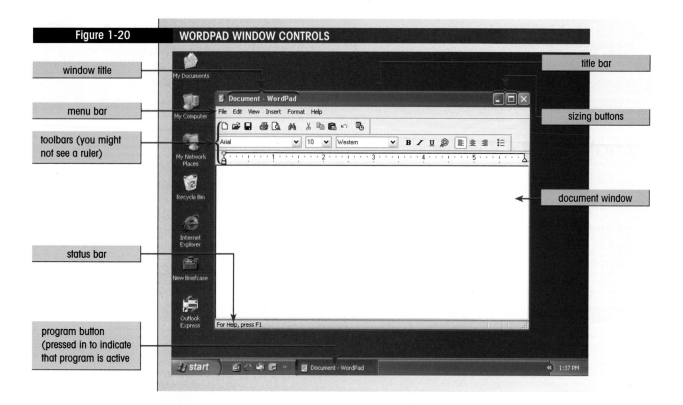

Figure 1-20   **WORDPAD WINDOW CONTROLS**

window title

menu bar

toolbars (you might not see a ruler)

status bar

program button (pressed in to indicate that program is active

title bar

sizing buttons

document window

Manipulating a Window

On the right side of the title bar are three buttons. You are already familiar with the Close button. The Minimize button, the first of the three buttons, hides a window so that only its program button is visible on the taskbar. The other button changes name and function depending on the status of the window. (It either maximizes the window or restores it to a predefined size.) Figure 1-21 shows how these buttons work.

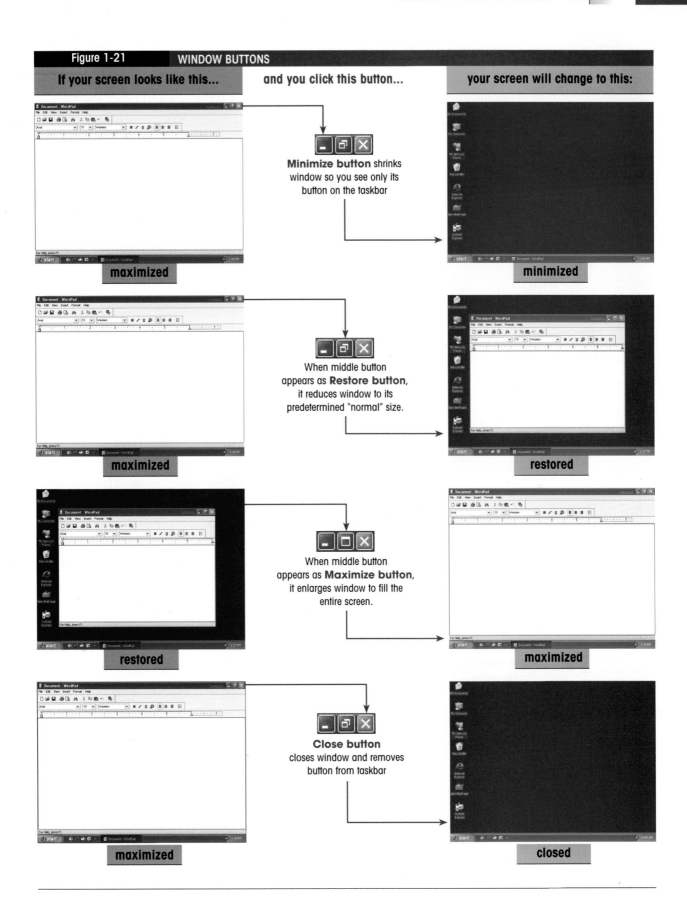

Figure 1-21 WINDOW BUTTONS

Minimizing a Window

The Minimize button hides a window so that only the program button on the taskbar remains visible. You can use the Minimize button when you want to hide a window temporarily but keep the program running.

To minimize the WordPad window:

1. Click the **Minimize** button ▣ on the WordPad title bar. The WordPad window reduces so that only the Document - WordPad button on the taskbar is visible.

   TROUBLE? If you accidentally clicked the Close button and closed the WordPad program window, use the Start button to start WordPad again, and then repeat Step 1.

Redisplaying a Window

You can redisplay a minimized window by clicking the program's button on the taskbar. When you redisplay a window, it becomes the active window.

To redisplay the WordPad window:

1. Click the **Document - WordPad** button on the taskbar. The WordPad window is restored to its previous size. The Document - WordPad button looks pushed in— a visual clue that WordPad is now the active window.

   The taskbar button provides another means of switching between a window's minimized and active states.

2. Click the **Document – WordPad** button on the taskbar again to minimize the window.

3. Click the **Document – WordPad** button once more to redisplay the window.

Maximizing a Window

The Maximize button enlarges a window so that it fills the entire screen. You will probably do most of your work using maximized windows because they allow you to see more of your program and data.

To maximize the WordPad window:

1. Click the **Maximize** button ▣ on the WordPad title bar.

   TROUBLE? If the window is already maximized, it will fill the entire screen, and the Maximize button won't appear. Instead, you'll see the Restore button ▣. Skip Step 1.

Restoring a Window

The Restore button reduces the window so that it is smaller than the entire screen. This feature is useful if you want to see more than one window at a time. Also, because the window is smaller, you can move the window to another location on the screen or change the dimensions of the window.

To restore a window:

1. Click the **Restore** button 🔲 on the WordPad title bar. Notice that once a window is restored, 🔲 changes to the Maximize button 🔲.

Moving a Window

You can use the mouse to move a window to a new position on the screen. When you click an object and then press and hold down the mouse button while moving the mouse, you are **dragging** the object. You can move an object on the screen by dragging it to a new location. If you want to move a window, you drag the window by its title bar. You cannot move a maximized window.

To drag the WordPad window to a new location:

1. Position the mouse pointer on the WordPad title bar.

2. Press and hold down the left mouse button, and then move the mouse up or down a little to drag the window. The window moves as you move the mouse.

3. Position the window anywhere on the desktop, and then release the left mouse button. The WordPad window appears in the new location.

4. Drag the WordPad window to the upper-left corner of the desktop.

Changing the Size of a Window

You can also use the mouse to change the size of a window. Notice the sizing handle 🔳 at the lower-right corner of the window. The **sizing handle** provides a visible control for changing the size of a window.

To change the size of the WordPad window:

1. Position the pointer over the sizing handle 🔳. The pointer changes to ↖↘. See Figure 1-22.

Figure 1-22   PREPARING TO RESIZE A WINDOW

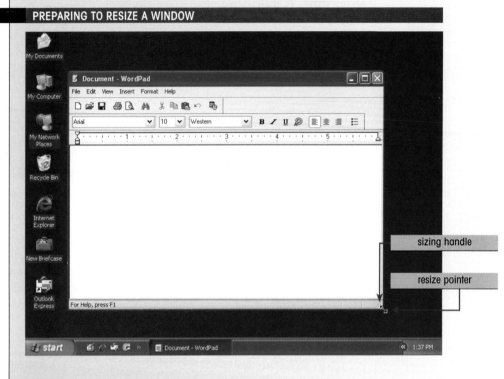

2. Press and hold down the mouse button, and then drag the sizing handle down and to the right.

3. Release the mouse button. Now the window is larger.

4. Practice using the sizing handle to make the WordPad window larger or smaller, and then maximize the WordPad window.

You can also drag the window borders left, right, up, or down to change a window's size.

Using Program Menus

Most Windows programs use menus to organize the program's features and available functions. The menu bar is typically located at the top of the program window and shows the names of the menus, such as File, Edit, and Help. Windows XP menus are relatively standard—most programs designed for Windows include similar menus. Learning new programs is easy because you can make a pretty good guess about which menu contains the task you want to perform.

Selecting Options from a Menu

When you click any menu name, the choices for that menu appear below the menu bar. These choices are referred to as **menu items** or **commands**. To select a menu item, you click it. For example, the File menu, a standard menu in most Windows programs, contains the items and commands typically related to working with a file: creating, opening, saving, and printing.

To select the Page Setup menu command from the File menu:

1. Click **File** on the WordPad menu bar to open the File menu. See Figure 1-23.

Figure 1-23	FILE MENU

your menu may show additional options

Page Setup command

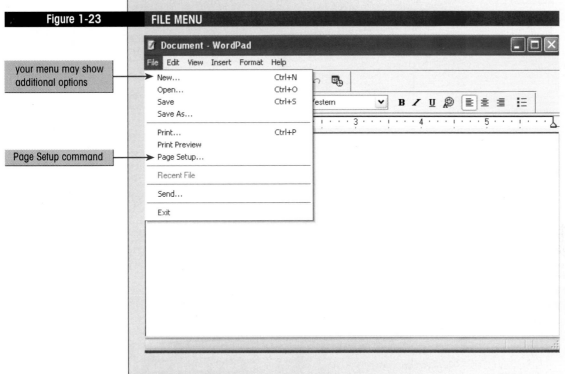

TROUBLE? If you open a menu and then decide not to select any of its commands, you can close the menu by clicking its name again.

2. Click **Page Setup** to open the Page Setup dialog box. A **dialog box** is a special kind of window where you enter or choose settings for how you want to perform a task. You use the Page Setup dialog box to set margins and some printing options.

TROUBLE? If a printer has not been installed for your computer, a message appears indicating that you must install a printer. (Click the Yes button, and then ask your instructor or technical support person for help with installing a printer.)

3. After examining the dialog box, click the **OK** button to close the Page Setup dialog box.

TROUBLE? If you close WordPad by mistake, restart it.

Not all menu items and commands immediately carry out an action—some show sub-menus or ask you for more information about what you want to do. The menu gives you visual hints about what to expect when you select an item. These hints are sometimes referred to as **menu conventions**. Figure 1-24 shows examples of these menu conventions.

Figure 1-24	EXAMPLES OF MENU CONVENTIONS

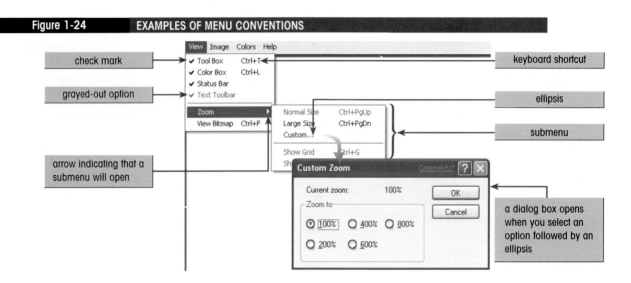

Figure 1-25 describes the Windows XP menu conventions.

Figure 1-25	MENU CONVENTIONS
CONVENTION	**DESCRIPTION**
Check mark	Indicates a toggle, or "on-off" switch (like a light switch) that is either checked (turned on) or not checked (turned off).
Ellipsis	Three dots that indicate you must make additional selections after you select that option. Options without dots do not require additional choices—they take effect as soon as you click them. If an option is followed by an ellipsis, a dialog box opens that allows you to enter specifications for how you want a task carried out.
Triangular arrow	Indicates the presence of a submenu. When you point at a menu option that has a triangular arrow, a submenu automatically appears.
Grayed-out option	Option that is not currently available. For example, a graphics program might display the Text Toolbar option in gray if there is no text in the graphic to work with.
Keyboard shortcut	A key or combination of keys that you can press to select the menu option without actually opening the menu.

Using Toolbars

Although you can usually perform all program commands by using menus, you also have one-click access to frequently used commands on the toolbars in the program window. You can quickly access common commands using the buttons on the toolbars. As task-related menu items and commands provided on menus, the buttons on a toolbar are also grouped and organized by tasks.

In Session 1.1 you learned that Windows XP programs often display ScreenTips, which indicate the purpose and function of a window component, for example, a button. Explore the WordPad toolbar buttons by looking at their ScreenTips.

To determine the names and descriptions of the buttons on the WordPad toolbar:

1. Position the pointer over any button on the toolbar, for example, the Print Preview button 🔍. After a short pause, the ScreenTip for the button appears below the button, and a description of the button appears in the status bar just above the Start button. See Figure 1-26.

Figure 1-26	TOOLBAR BUTTON AIDS

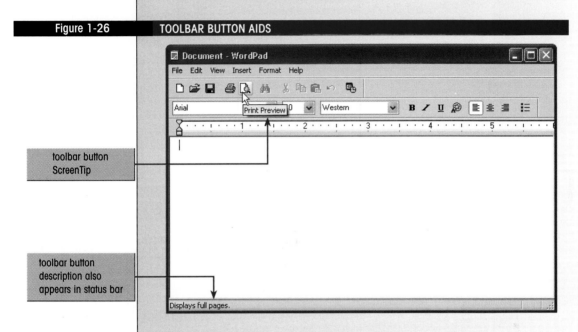

toolbar button ScreenTip

toolbar button description also appears in status bar

2. Move the pointer to each button on the toolbar to display its name and purpose.

To perform a command, you select the toolbar button by clicking it. When you pointed to each button on the WordPad toolbar, you found one called the Undo button. Clicking the Undo button reverses the effects of your last action.

To use the Undo button on the toolbar:

1. Type your name in the WordPad window.

2. Click the **Undo** button 🔄 on the toolbar. WordPad reverses your last action by removing your name from the WordPad window.

Using List Boxes and Scroll Bars

As you might guess from its name, a **list box** displays a list of available choices from which you can select. In WordPad, you can choose a date and time format from the Available formats list box in the Date/Time dialog box. List box controls usually include arrow buttons, a scroll bar, and a scroll box.

To use a list box in the Date/Time dialog box:

1. Click the **Date/Time** button ⬚ on the toolbar to open the Date and Time dialog box. See Figure 1-27.

Figure 1-27	DATE AND TIME DIALOG BOX

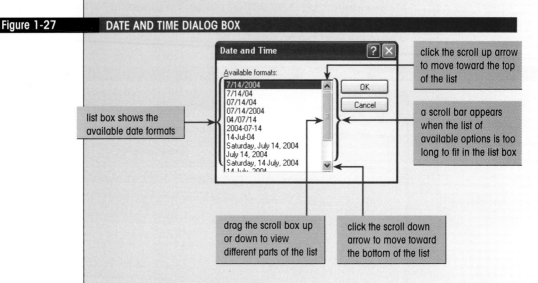

list box shows the available date formats

click the scroll up arrow to move toward the top of the list

a scroll bar appears when the list of available options is too long to fit in the list box

drag the scroll box up or down to view different parts of the list

click the scroll down arrow to move toward the bottom of the list

2. To scroll down the list, click the **scroll down arrow** button until you see the bottom of the list.

3. Drag the **scroll box** to the top of the scroll bar. Notice how the list scrolls back to the beginning.

TROUBLE? To drag the scroll box up, point to the scroll box, press and hold down the mouse button, and then move the mouse up.

4. Find a date format similar to "July 14, 2004" in the Available formats list box, and then click that date format to select it.

5. Click the **OK** button to close the Date and Time dialog box. The current date is inserted in your document.

A list box is helpful because it includes only options that are appropriate for your current task. For example, you can select only dates and times in the available formats from the list box in the Date and Time dialog box—no matter which format you choose, WordPad will recognize it. Sometimes, however, a list might not include every possible option, so it lets you type the option you want to select. In this case, the list box includes a **list arrow** on its right side. You can click the list arrow to view options and then select one, or you can type appropriate text.

Buttons can also have list arrows. The list arrow indicates that there is more than one option for that button. Rather than crowding the window with lots of buttons, one for each possible option, including a list arrow on a button organizes its options logically and compactly. Toolbars often include list boxes and buttons with list arrows. For example, the Font Size list box on the WordPad toolbar includes a list arrow. To select an option other than the one shown in the list box or on the button, you click the list arrow and then click the option that you want to use.

To select a new font size from the Font Size list box:

1. Click the **list arrow** for the Font Size list box on the toolbar. See Figure 1-28.

Figure 1-28	FONT SIZE LIST ARROW

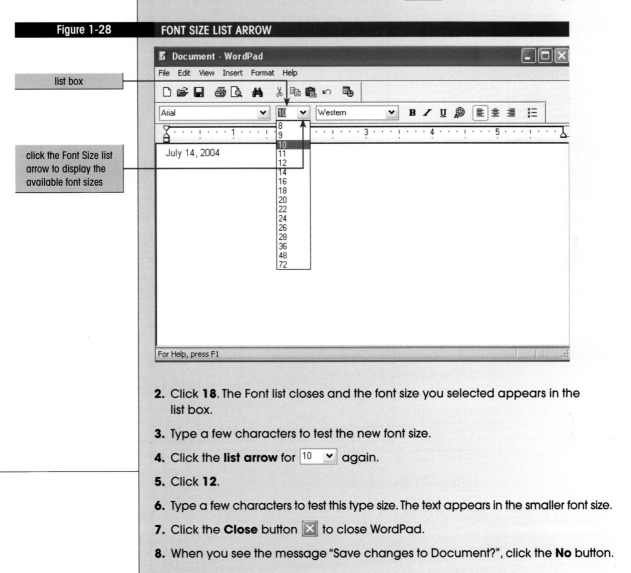

list box

click the Font Size list arrow to display the available font sizes

2. Click **18**. The Font list closes and the font size you selected appears in the list box.

3. Type a few characters to test the new font size.

4. Click the **list arrow** for again.

5. Click **12**.

6. Type a few characters to test this type size. The text appears in the smaller font size.

7. Click the **Close** button to close WordPad.

8. When you see the message "Save changes to Document?", click the **No** button.

Using Dialog Box Controls

Recall that when you select a menu command or item followed by an ellipsis, a dialog box opens that allows you to provide more information about how a program should carry out a task. Some dialog boxes group different kinds of information into bordered rectangular areas called **panes**. Within these panes, you will usually find tabs, option buttons, check boxes, and other controls that the program uses to collect information about how you want it to perform a task. Figure 1-29 displays examples of common dialog box controls.

Figure 1-29	EXAMPLES OF DIALOG BOX CONTROL

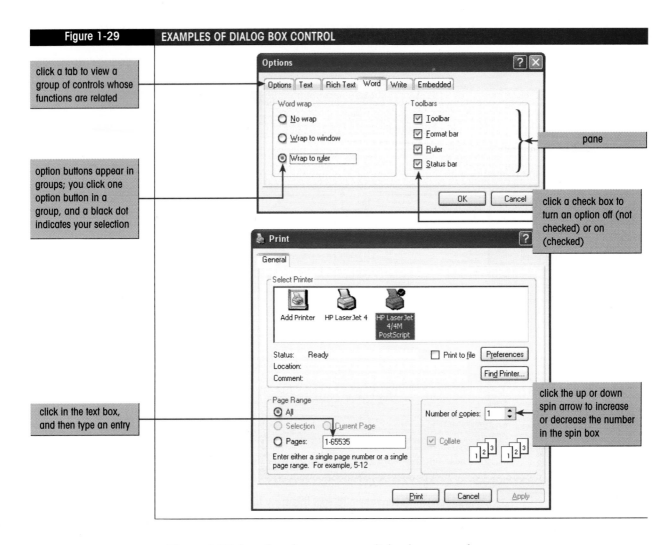

click a tab to view a group of controls whose functions are related

option buttons appear in groups; you click one option button in a group, and a black dot indicates your selection

click in the text box, and then type an entry

pane

click a check box to turn an option off (not checked) or on (checked)

click the up or down spin arrow to increase or decrease the number in the spin box

Figure 1-30 describes these common dialog box controls.

Figure 1-30	DESCRIPTION OF DIALOG BOX CONTROLS

CONTROL	DESCRIPTION
Tabs	Modeled after the tabs on file folders, tab controls are often used as containers for other Windows XP controls such as list boxes, option buttons, and check boxes. Click the appropriate tabs to view different pages of information or choices.
Option buttons	Also called radio buttons, option buttons allow you to select a single option from among one or more options.
Check boxes	Click a check box to select or deselect it; when it is selected, a check mark appears, indicating that the option is turned on; when deselected, the check box is blank and the option is off. When check boxes appear in groups, you can select or deselect as many as you want; they are not mutually exclusive, as option buttons are.
Spin boxes	Allow you to scroll easily through a set of numbers to choose the setting you want
Text boxes	Boxes into which you type additional information

Using Help

Windows XP **Help** provides on-screen information about the program you are using. Help for the Windows XP operating system is available by clicking the Start button on the taskbar, and then selecting Help and Support from the Start menu. If you want Help for a particular program, such as WordPad, you must first start the program and then click Help on the program's menu bar.

When you start Help for Windows XP, a Windows Help and Support Center window opens, giving you access to Help files stored on your computer as well as Help information stored on Microsoft's Web site. If you are not connected to the Web, you only have access to the Help files stored on your computer.

To start Windows XP Help:

1. Click the **Start** button _start_ on the taskbar.

2. Click **Help and Support**. The Help and Support Center window opens. See Figure 1-31.

   TROUBLE? If the Help and Support window does not display the information you see in Figure 1-31, click the Home icon on the navigation bar to view Help contents. The navigation bar is located at the top of the window.

Figure 1-31	WINDOWS XP HELP AND SUPPORT CENTER WINDOW

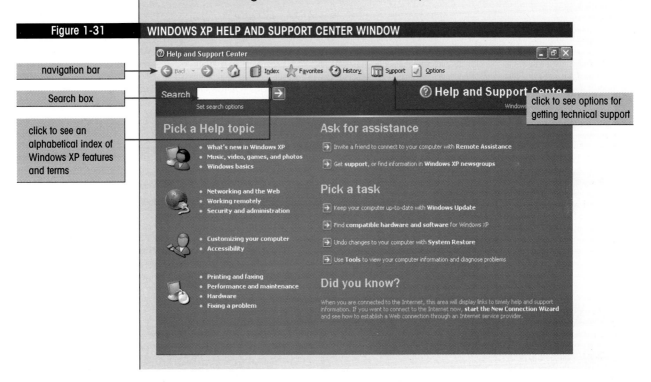

The Windows XP Help and Support window organizes the vast amount of help and support information into **pages**. These six pages of information—the Home, Index, Favorites, History, Support, and Options pages—are designed to aid users in locating help on a particular topic quickly. To open one of these pages, click its icon on the navigation bar. The **Home page** lists common tasks under the heading "Pick a Help topic" in the left pane on the page. Click a task to see detailed information or instructions about that task in the right pane of the page. The right pane of the Home page lists common tasks, tips, and ways you can ask for assistance. For example, you can contact a support professional or download the latest version of Windows XP. The **Index** page displays an alphabetical list of all the Help topics from which you can choose. The **Favorites** page shows Help topics you've added to your Favorites list. To add a topic to the Favorites list, open the topic, and then click the

Favorites button on the Help window. The **History** page lists links you've recently selected in Help. The **Support** page includes links that you can click to connect to the Microsoft Web site, if possible, for additional assistance. The **Options** page provides ways you can customize Help. For example, you can change the appearance of the navigation bar.

If you cannot find the topic you want listed on any of the six Help and Support Services pages, the word that you are using for a feature or topic might differ from the word that Windows XP uses. You can use the **Search box** to search for all keywords contained in the Help pages, not just the topic titles. In the Search box, you can type any word or phrase, click the Start Searching button, and Windows XP lists all the Help topics that contain that word or phrase.

Viewing Topics on the Windows XP Help and Support Center Home Page

Windows XP Help includes instructions on using Help itself. You can learn how to find a Help topic by using the Help and Support Center Home page.

To use the Help and Support Center Home page:

1. On the Home page, click **Windows basics**. A list of topics related to using Windows XP appears in the left pane of the Help and Support Center window.

2. Click **Tips for using Help**. A list of Help topics appears in the right pane of the Help window.

3. Click **Change fonts in Help and Support Center**. The instructions appear in the right pane of the Help and Support Center window, as shown in Figure 1-32.

Figure 1-32   **FINDING A HELP TOPIC ON THE HOME PAGE**

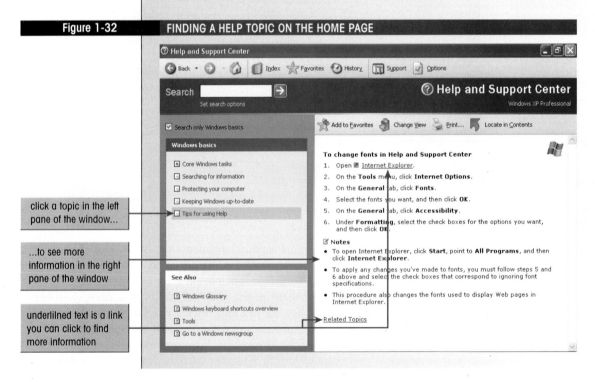

click a topic in the left pane of the window...

...to see more information in the right pane of the window

underlilned text is a link you can click to find more information

Besides listing the pages in the Help and Support Center window, the navigation bar contains two buttons—the Back button ⬅ and the Forward button ➡. You use these buttons to navigate the pages you've already opened. You'll use the Back button next to return to the previous page you viewed. Once you do, you activate the Forward button, which you can click to go to the next page of those you've opened.

4. Click the **Back** button ⬅. You return to the Tips for using Help page.

Selecting a Topic from the Index

The Index page allows you to jump to a Help topic by selecting a topic from an indexed list. For example, you can use the Index page to learn how to arrange open windows on your desktop.

To find a Help topic using the Index page:

1. On the navigation bar, click **Index** 🗋. A long list of indexed Help topics displays in the left pane.

2. Drag the **scroll box** down to view additional topics in the list box.

   You can quickly jump to any part of the list by typing the first few characters of a word or phrase in the box that appears above the Index list.

3. If necessary, click in the **Type in the keyword to find** text box above the Index list, and then type **windows**. As you type each character in the word, the list of Index topic scrolls and eventually displays topics that relate to windows.

4. Under the "windows and panes on your computer screen" topic, click the topic **reducing windows to taskbar buttons**, and then click the **Display** button. When there is just one topic, it appears immediately in the right pane; otherwise, the Topics Found window opens, listing all topics indexed under the entry that interests you.

   The information you requested displays in the right pane. See Figure 1-33. Notice this topic has two underlined phrases, "taskbar" and "Related Topics." You can click underlined words or phrases to view definitions or additional information.

Figure 1-33

USING THE INDEX TO LOCATE INFORMATION

type some or all of the characters in the word you want to look up in the index

click to display more information about the selected topic

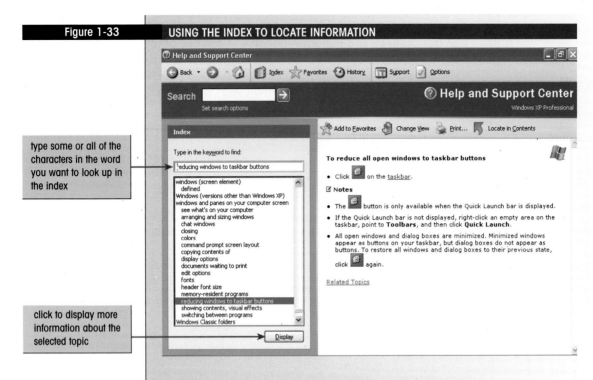

5. Click the underlined phrase **taskbar**. A ScreenTip shows the definition of "taskbar." See Figure 1-34.

Figure 1-34

VIEWING ADDITIONAL INFORMATION

click an underlined word to view a definition or additional information

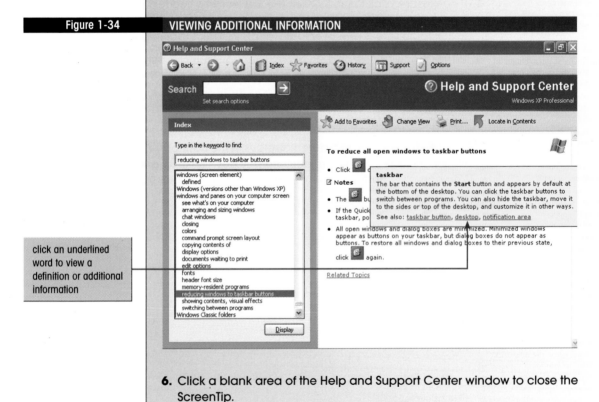

6. Click a blank area of the Help and Support Center window to close the ScreenTip.

If you have an Internet connection, you can use another Help page, Support, to contact Microsoft Support or get in touch with other users of Windows XP. The Support page works like the Home page. To get support on a particular feature, you click a support option and then click the topic for which you need help. Continue clicking topics, if necessary, until you get help from a Microsoft support person or an experienced Windows XP user.

Searching the Help Pages

If you can't find the topic you need by using the Home or Index pages, or if you want to quickly find Help pages related to a particular topic, you can use the Search box. Suppose you want to know how to exit Windows XP, but you don't know if Windows refers to this as exiting, quitting, closing, or shutting down. You can search the Help pages to find just the right topic.

To search the Help pages for information on exiting Windows XP:

1. Click in the Search box. A blinking insertion point appears.

2. Type **shutdown** and then click the **Start Searching** button ➡. A list of Help pages containing the word "shutdown" displays in the left pane of the Help and Support window. The ones listed under Suggested Topics are topics where "shutdown" has been assigned as a keyword—meaning the topics have to do with shutting something down.

3. Click the **Full-text Search Matches** button. The text of these topics includes the word *shutdown*.

4. Click the **Suggested Topics** button, and then click **Turn off the computer**. A Help topic displays in the right pane of the Help and Support Center window, as shown in Figure 1-35.

| Figure 1-35 | USING SEARCH TO FIND A HELP PAGE |

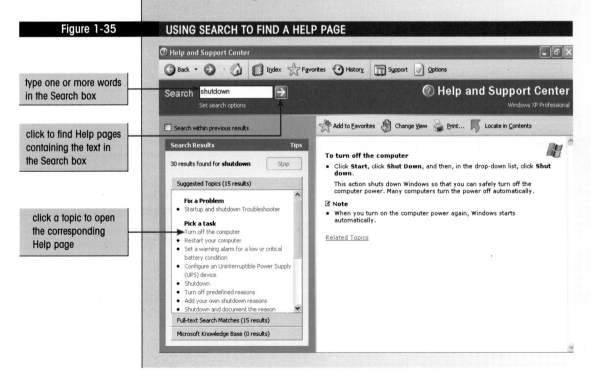

type one or more words in the Search box

click to find Help pages containing the text in the Search box

click a topic to open the corresponding Help page

If the text of this topic were longer than the Help and Support Center window, you could use the scroll bar to read all the text.

5. Click the **Close** button ⊠ to close the Help and Support Center window.

Now that you know how Windows XP Help works, don't forget to use it! Use Help when you need to perform a new task or when you forget how to complete a procedure.

You've finished the tutorial, and as you shut down Windows XP, Steve returns from class. You take a moment to tell him all you've learned: you know how to start and close programs and how to use multiple programs at the same time. You have learned how to work with windows and the controls they employ. Finally, you've learned how to get help when you need it. Steve congratulates you and comments that you are well on your way to mastering the fundamentals of using the Windows XP operating system.

Session 1.2 QUICK CHECK

1. What is the difference between the title bar and a toolbar?

2. Provide the name and purpose of each button:
    a. ▭   **b.** ▢   **c.** ⧉   **d.** ⊠

3. Explain each of the following menu conventions:
    a. Ellipsis (...)
    b. Grayed-out
    c. ▷
    d. ✔

4. A (n) _____ consists of a group of buttons, each of which provides one-click access to important program functions.

5. What is the purpose of the scroll bar?

6. Option buttons allow you to select _____ option(s) at a time.

7. To learn how to perform new tasks, you can use _____.

REVIEW ASSIGNMENTS

Case 1. Running Two Programs and Switching Between Them In this tutorial you learned how to run more than one program at a time, using WordPad and Paint. You can run other programs at the same time, too. Complete the following steps, and write your answers to Questions b through f:

   a. Start the computer. Enter your username and password if prompted to do so.
   b. Click the Start button. How many menu options are on the Start menu?

Explore
   c. Run the Calculator program located on the Accessories menu. How many program buttons are now on the taskbar? (Don't count toolbar buttons or items in the notification area.)
   d. Run the Paint program and maximize the Paint window. How many programs are running now?
   e. Switch to Calculator. What are two visual clues that tell you that Calculator is the active program?

Explore

    f. Multiply 576 by 1457 using the Calculator accessory. (*Hint*: Click the numbers and arithmetic operators on the Calculator keypad.) What is the result?

    g. Close Calculator and then close Paint.

Explore

Case 2. WordPad Help In Tutorial 1 you learned how to use Windows XP Help. Just about every Windows XP program has a Help feature. Many computer users can learn to use a program just by using Help. To use Help, you start the program and then click the Help menu at the top of the program window. Try using WordPad Help:

    a. Start WordPad.

    b. Click Help on the menu bar, and then click Help Topics.

    c. The Index tab in WordPad Help works like the Index page in Windows XP Help. Using the Index tab in WordPad Help, write out your answers to Questions 1 through 4.

        1. How do you create a bulleted list?

        2. How do you set the page margins in a document?

        3. How do you undo a mistake?

        4. How do you change the font style of a block of text?

    d. Close Help and then close WordPad.

Case 3. The Index Page versus the Search Box You might have heard that Windows XP makes it possible to speak to your computer and have it carry out your voice commands. This feature is called **speech recognition**. You could browse through the Help and Support Home page, although you might not know where to look to find information about speech recognition. You could also use the Index page to search through the indexed entries. Or you could use the Search box to find all Help topics that mention speech recognition.

    a. Start Windows XP Help and use the Index page to find information about the topic of speech recognition. How many topics are listed? What is their primary subject matter?

    b. Use the Search box to find information about the topic of speech recognition. How many topics are listed?

    c. Write a paragraph comparing the two lists of topics. You don't have to view them all, but in your paragraph, indicate which tab seems to yield more information. Close the Help and Support Center window.

Case 4. Discover Windows XP Windows XP Help lets you access articles that provide more detailed information about common features or introduce new features. You can find and read an article about one new feature Windows XP offers—playing music and making music CDs on your computer.

    a. Start Windows XP Help, open the Home page, click What's new in Windows XP, and then click Windows XP Articles: Walkthrough ways to use your PC.

    b. Click Walkthrough: Making Music.

    c. Read the Getting Started page. Note that the box in the upper-left corner of the window lists the contents of the article. Each topic is a link you can click to go to another page in the article.

    d. Click the links in the contents box, and then answer the following questions using the information you find:

        1. How can you listen to music using Windows XP?

        2. What is a playlist? What is the first step you take to create one?

        3. What is the advantage of listening to the Internet radio?

    e. Close Help and then close WordPad.

PROJECTS

1. Many types of pointing devices are on the market today. Research the types of available devices. Consider what devices are appropriate for these situations: desktop or laptop computers, connected or remote devices, and ergonomic or standard designs. (Look up the term *ergonomic*.)

    To locate information, use up-to-date computer books, trade computer magazines (such as *PC Computing* and *PC Magazine*), or the Internet (if you know how). Your instructor might suggest specific resources you can use. Write a one-page report describing the types of devices available, the differing needs of users, special features that make pointing devices more useful, price comparisons. Finally, indicate what you would choose if you needed to buy a pointing device.

2. Locate information about the release of Windows XP, using the resources available to you, either through your library or the Internet (if you know how). Trade computer magazines are an excellent source of information about software. Read several articles about Windows XP, and then write a one-page essay discussing the features that seem most important to the people who evaluate the software. If you find reviews of the software, mention the features to which reviewers had the strongest reaction, pro or con.

3. **Upgrading** is the process of placing a more recent version of a product onto your computer. When Windows XP first came out, people had to decide whether they wanted to upgrade their computers to Windows XP. Interview at least three people you know who are well-informed Windows computer users. Ask them whether they use Windows XP or an older version of Windows. If they use an older version, ask why they chose not to upgrade. If they use Windows XP, ask why they chose to upgrade. Ask such questions as:
   a. What features convinced you to upgrade or made you decide to wait?
   b. What role did the price of the upgrade play?
   c. Would you or did you have to purchase new hardware to make the upgrade? How did this affect your decision?
   d. If you did upgrade, are you happy with that decision? If you didn't, do you intend to upgrade in the near future? Why or why not?
   Write a single-page essay summarizing what you learned from these interviews about making the decision to upgrade.

4. Choose a topic you'd like to research using the Windows XP online Help system. Look for information on your topic using the Help and Support Home page, Index page, and Search box. Once you find all the information you can, compare the three methods (Home page, Index page, Search box) of looking for information. Write a paragraph that discusses which method proved most useful. Did you reach the same information topics using all three methods? In a second paragraph, summarize what you learned about your topic. Finally, in a third paragraph, indicate under what circumstances you'd use which method.

LAB ASSIGNMENTS

Using a Keyboard To become an effective computer user, you must be familiar with your primary input device—the keyboard. See the Read This Before You Begin page for information on installing and starting the lab.

1. The Steps for the Using a Keyboard Lab provides you with a structured introduction to the keyboard's layout and the functions of special computer keys. Click the Steps button and begin the steps. As you work through the Steps, answer all of the Quick Check questions that appear. When you complete the steps, you will see a Summary Report of your performance on the Quick Checks. Follow the directions on the screen to print the Summary Report.

2. You can develop your typing skills using the typing tutor in Explore. Start the typing tutor in Explore. Take the typing test and print your results.

3. In Explore, try to increase your typing speed by 10 words per minute. For example, if you currently type 20 words per minute, your goal is 30 words per minute. Practice each typing lesson until you see a message indicating that you can proceed to the next lesson. Create a Practice Record, as shown here, to keep track of how much you practice. When you reach your goal, print the results of a typing test to verify your results.

Practice Record

Name:

Section:

Start Date: Start Typing Speed: wpm

End Date: End Typing Speed: wpm

Lesson #:   Date Practiced/Time Practiced

Using a Mouse A mouse is a standard input device on most of today's computers. You need to know how to use a mouse to manipulate graphical user interfaces and to use the rest of the Labs. See the Read This Before You Begin page for information on installing and starting the lab.

1. The Steps for the Using a Mouse Lab show you how to click, double-click, and drag objects using the mouse. Click the Steps button and begin the steps. As you work through the steps, answer all Quick Check questions that appear. When you complete the steps, you will see a Summary Report of your performance on the Quick Checks. Follow the directions on the screen to print the Summary Report.

2. In Explore, create a poster to demonstrate your ability to use a mouse and to control a Windows program. To create a poster for an upcoming sports event, select a graphic, type the caption for the poster, and then select a font, font styles, and a border. Print your completed poster.

QUICK | CHECK ANSWERS

Session 1.1

1. The taskbar contains buttons that give you access to commands and programs.

2. multitasking

3. Start menu

4. Lift up the mouse and move it to the right.

5. Its button appears on the taskbar.

6. to conserve computer resources such as memory

7. to ensure you don't lose data and damage your files

Session 1.2

1. The title bar identifies the window and contains window controls; toolbars contain buttons that provide you with shortcuts to common menu commands.

2. **a.** The Minimize button shrinks the window so you see its button on the taskbar.
 b. The Maximize button enlarges the window to fill the entire screen.
 c. The Restore button reduces the window to a predetermined size.
 d. The Close button closes the window and removes the program button from the taskbar.

3. **a.** Ellipsis indicates a dialog box will open.
 b. Grayed out indicates that the option is not currently available.
 c. Arrow indicates that a submenu will open.
 d. Check mark indicates a toggle option.

4. toolbar

5. Scroll bars appear when the contents of a box or window are too long to fit; you drag the scroll box to view different parts of the contents.

6. one

7. online Help

OBJECTIVES

In this tutorial you will:

- Format a disk
- Enter, select, insert, and delete text
- Create and save a file
- Open, edit, and print a file
- View the list of files on your Data Disk and change view options
- Navigate a hierarchy of folders
- Move, copy, delete, and rename a file
- Make a copy of your Data Disk

LAB

Using Files

WORKING WITH FILES

Creating, Saving, and Managing Files

CASE

Distance Learning

You recently purchased a computer to gain new skills and stay competitive in the job market. You hope to use the computer to enroll in a few distance learning courses. **Distance learning** is formalized education that typically takes place using a computer and the Internet, replacing normal classroom interaction with modern communications technology. Distance learning instructors often make their course material available on the **World Wide Web**, also called the **Web**. The Web is a network of **Web pages**, which are electronic documents stored on the Internet that people can access and explore using **hyperlinks**. Hyperlinks are text or graphical elements embedded in the Web pages. You click the hyperlinks in a Web page to navigate to related Web pages and **Web sites**, computers connected to the Internet that store collections of Web pages.

Your computer came with the Windows XP operating system already installed. Your friend Shannon suggests that before you enroll in any online course, you should become more comfortable with your computer and with Windows XP. Knowing how to save, locate, and organize your files will make the time you spend working with your computer much more productive. A **file** is a collection of data that has a name and is stored on a computer. Once you create a file, you can open it, edit its contents, print it, and save it again—usually using the same program you used to create it.

In this tutorial, you will learn how to perform some basic tasks in Windows XP programs, such as formatting a disk and working with text and files. You will also learn how to view information on your computer in different ways. Finally, you'll spend time learning how to organize your files.

SESSION 2.1

In Session 2.1 you will format a disk so you can store files on it. You will create, save, open, and print a file. You will learn more about the difference between the insertion point and the mouse pointer. You also will learn the basic skills for working with text, such as entering, selecting, inserting, and deleting text. For the steps in this tutorial, you will need two blank 3½" disks.

Formatting a Disk

Before you can save files on a disk, the disk must be formatted. When the computer **formats** a disk, the magnetic particles on the disk's surface are arranged so data can be stored on the disk. Today, many disks are sold preformatted and can be used right out of the box. However, if you purchase an unformatted disk or if you have an old disk you want to completely erase and reuse, you can format the disk using the Windows XP Format command. This command is available through the **My Computer window**, a feature of Windows XP that you use to view, organize, and access the programs, files, and drives on your computer. You open My Computer by using its icon on the desktop. You'll learn more about the My Computer window in Session 2.2.

The following steps explain how to format a 3½" high-density disk using drive A. Your instructor will explain how to revise the instructions given in these steps if the procedure is different for your lab equipment.

Make sure you are using a blank disk (or one that contains data you no longer need) before you perform these steps.

To format a disk:

1. Start Windows XP and log on using your user name, if necessary.

2. Write your name on the label of a 3½-inch disk, and then insert your disk in drive A. See Figure 2-1.

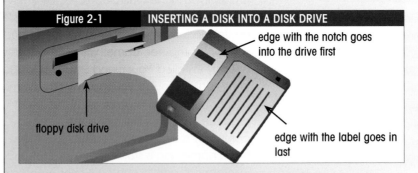

Figure 2-1   INSERTING A DISK INTO A DISK DRIVE

edge with the notch goes into the drive first

floppy disk drive

edge with the label goes in last

TROUBLE? If your disk does not fit in drive A, put it in drive B, and then substitute drive B for drive A in all of the steps for the rest of the tutorial.

3. Double-click the **My Computer** icon on the desktop. See Figure 2-2. The My Computer window on your screen might be maximized.

TROUBLE? If you see a list of items instead of icons like those in Figure 2-2, click View on the My Computer menu bar, and then click Tiles. Your toolbar may not exactly match the one in Figure 2-2; it may have fewer or more buttons.

Figure 2-2   **MY COMPUTER WINDOW**

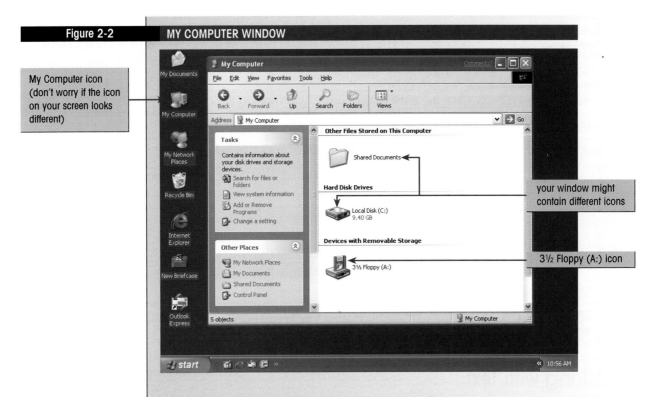

My Computer icon (don't worry if the icon on your screen looks different)

your window might contain different icons

3½ Floppy (A:) icon

4. Right-click the **3½ Floppy (A:)** icon to open its shortcut menu, and then click **Format**. The Format 3½ Floppy (A:) dialog box opens. See Figure 2-3.

Figure 2-3   **FORMATTING A FLOPPY DISK**

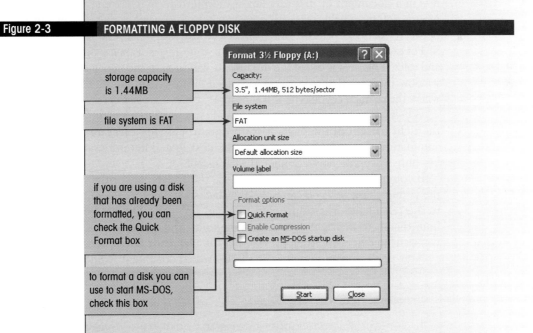

storage capacity is 1.44MB

file system is FAT

if you are using a disk that has already been formatted, you can check the Quick Format box

to format a disk you can use to start MS-DOS, check this box

5. Make sure your dialog box settings match those in Figure 2-3. These settings describe a disk's characteristics and format options. The capacity of a floppy disk indicates how much data it can hold—a 3½-inch floppy disk can hold 1.44MB of data. By default, Windows XP uses the FAT (File Allocation Table) file system for floppy disks. A **file system** is the way files are organized on the disk. Windows XP supports other file systems such as FAT32 and NTFS. Selecting a file system, allocation unit size, volume label, and creating an MS-DOS startup disk are advanced topics, so you can accept the defaults for these options. If you have a disk that has been previously formatted, and you're sure the disk is not damaged, you can use the Quick Format option. In this instance, you will do a full format, so this box should remain unchecked.

6. Click the **Start** button to begin formatting the disk.

TROUBLE? If you are using a disk that contains data, you will see a warning that formatting will erase all the data on the disk. Click OK to continue.

A bar at the bottom of the Format window shows you how the formatting is progressing.

7. When the formatting is completed, a Format Complete message box appears. Click the **OK** button.

8. Click the **Close** button to close the Format 3½ Floppy (A:) dialog box, and then close the My Computer window to return to the desktop.

Now that you have formatted a disk, you can create a document and save it as a file on your disk. To create a document, you first need to learn how to enter text into a document.

Working with Text

To accomplish many computing tasks, you need to type text where text is required, whether it is in a document or in a text box. Entering text involves first learning how to place the mouse pointer so the text will appear where you want it. Then you can insert new text between existing words or sentences, select text, and delete text.

For example, when you start WordPad, a white area will appear below the menu bar, toolbars, and ruler. This area is called the **document window**. In the upper-left corner of the document window, there is a flashing vertical bar, called the **insertion point**. The insertion point indicates where the characters you type will appear.

When you type sentences of text, you do not need to press the Enter key when you reach the right margin of the page. Most programs contain a feature called **word wrap**, which automatically continues your text on the next line. Therefore, you should press the Enter key only when you have completed a paragraph.

If you make a typing error, you can use the Delete key or the Backspace key. If you type the wrong character, you can press the **Backspace key** to delete the character immediately to the left of the insertion point. You can press the **Delete key** to delete the character immediately to the right of the insertion point. You can also use the mouse to select the text you want to delete and then press either the Delete or Backspace key.

Now you will type some text in the WordPad document window.

To type text in WordPad:

1. Start WordPad and locate the insertion point in the WordPad document window.

TROUBLE? If the WordPad window does not fill the screen, click the Maximize button 🔲 on the WordPad title bar.

TROUBLE? If you cannot find the insertion point, move the ⌶ pointer over the WordPad window and then click the mouse button. The insertion point will appear in the upper-left corner of the document window.

2. Type your name, just as you would on a typewriter, pressing the Shift key as you type uppercase letters and using the spacebar to enter spaces.

3. Press the **Enter** key to end the current paragraph and to move the insertion point down to the next line.

4. Type the following sentences, watching what happens when the insertion point reaches the right margin of the page:

This is a sample typed in WordPad. See what happens when the insertion point reaches the right edge of the page. Note how the text wraps automatically to the next line.

TROUBLE? If you make a mistake, delete the incorrect character(s) using the Backspace key or Delete key. Then type the correct character(s).

TROUBLE? If your text doesn't wrap, your screen might be set up to display more information than the screen used for the figures in this tutorial, or your WordPad program might not be set to use Word Wrap. To set the Word Wrap option, click View on the menu bar, click Options, click the Rich Text tab in the Options dialog box, click the Wrap to window option button, and then click the OK button.

The Insertion Point Versus the Pointer

The insertion point is not the same as the pointer. When the pointer is in the document window, the pointer is called the **I-beam pointer**. Figure 2-4 explains the difference between the insertion point and the I-beam pointer.

Figure 2-4	THE INSERTION POINT VS. THE POINTER

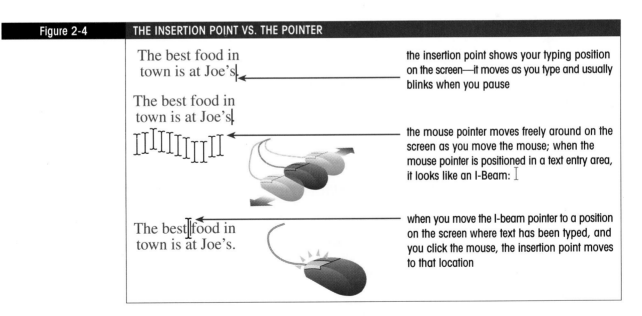

The best food in town is at Joe's | the insertion point shows your typing position on the screen—it moves as you type and usually blinks when you pause

The best food in town is at Joe's | the mouse pointer moves freely around on the screen as you move the mouse; when the mouse pointer is positioned in a text entry area, it looks like an I-Beam: I

The best food in town is at Joe's. | when you move the I-beam pointer to a position on the screen where text has been typed, and you click the mouse, the insertion point moves to that location

When you enter text, the insertion point moves as you type. If you want to enter text in a location other than where the insertion point is positioned, you can use the pointer to move the insertion point to a different location. Move the I-beam pointer to where you want to type, and then click. The insertion point moves to where you clicked. In most programs, the insertion point blinks so you can locate it easily on a screen filled with text.

Try moving the insertion point to different locations in the sample text in the WordPad document window.

To move the insertion point to a new location in the sample text:

1. Locate the insertion point and the I-beam pointer in the WordPad document window. The insertion point should be at the end of the sentence you typed in the last set of steps. The easiest way to find the I-beam pointer is to move your mouse gently until you see the pointer. The pointer will look like ⌖ until you move it into the document window; then the pointer will change to I.

2. Use your mouse to move the I-beam pointer just to the left of the word "sample," and then click. The insertion point should now be just to the left of the "s" in the word "sample."

   TROUBLE? If you have trouble clicking just to the left of the "s," try clicking in the word and then using the left arrow key to move the insertion point one character at a time.

3. Move the I-beam pointer to a blank area near the bottom of the document window, and then click. Notice the insertion point does not jump to the location of the I-beam pointer. Instead the insertion point jumps to the end of the last sentence or to the point in the bottom line directly above where you clicked. The insertion point can move only within existing text. In most programs, the insertion point cannot be moved out of the existing text.

Selecting Text

Many text-editing operations are performed on a **block of text**, which is one or more consecutive characters, words, sentences, or paragraphs. Once you select a block of text, you can delete it, move it, replace it, underline it, and so on. To deselect a block of text, click anywhere outside the selected block.

If you want to delete the phrase "See what happens" in the text you just typed and replace it with the phrase "You can watch word wrap in action," you do not have to delete the first phrase one character at a time. Instead, you can select the entire phrase and then type the replacement phrase.

To select and replace the block of text "See what happens":

1. Move the I-beam pointer just to the left of the word "See."

2. Click and then drag the I-beam pointer over the text to the end of the word "happens." The phrase "See what happens" should now be highlighted, indicating it is selected. See Figure 2-5.

   TROUBLE? If the space to the right of the word "happens" is also selected, that means your computer is set up to select spaces in addition to words. You can continue with Step 3.

Figure 2-5	SELECTING TEXT

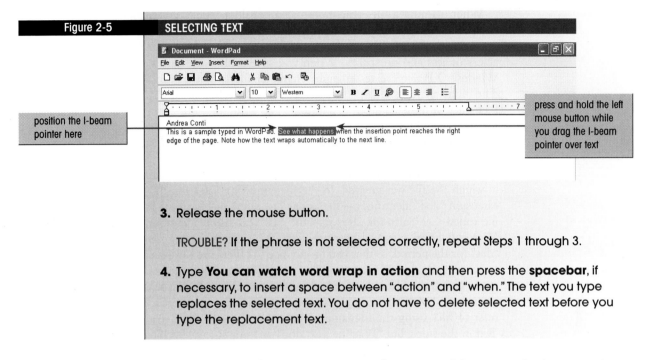

position the I-beam pointer here

press and hold the left mouse button while you drag the I-beam pointer over text

3. Release the mouse button.

TROUBLE? If the phrase is not selected correctly, repeat Steps 1 through 3.

4. Type **You can watch word wrap in action** and then press the **spacebar**, if necessary, to insert a space between "action" and "when." The text you type replaces the selected text. You do not have to delete selected text before you type the replacement text.

In addition to replacing existing text with new material, you can also insert text into an existing block of text.

Inserting Text

Windows XP programs usually operate in **insert mode**—when you type a new character, the characters to the right of the insertion point automatically move over to make room.

Insert the word "page" before the word "typed" in the sample text.

To insert text:

1. Position the insertion point just before the word "typed".

2. Type **page** and then press the **spacebar**. The letters in the first line are pushed to the right to make room for the new characters. When you insert text and a word is pushed past the right margin, the word wrap feature moves the word down to the beginning of the next line.

Now that you have practiced typing, you can save the file.

Saving a File

Using Files

As you type text, it is held temporarily in the computer's memory and is erased when you turn off or restart the computer. For permanent storage, you need to save your work on a disk. In the computer lab, you will probably save your work on a floppy disk in drive A.

When you save a file, you must give it a name, which then becomes its **filename**. Windows XP allows you to use up to 255 characters in a filename—this gives you plenty of room to name your file accurately so that you'll know the contents of the file just by looking at the filename. You can use spaces and certain punctuation symbols in your filenames. You cannot use the symbols \ / ? : * " < > | in a filename, but other symbols such as & ; - and $ are allowed.

When naming a file, you should also consider whether you might use your files on a computer that is running older programs. Programs designed for the Windows 3.1 or DOS operating systems (which were created before 1995) require that filenames have eight characters or less and no spaces. When you save a file with a long filename in Windows XP, Windows XP also creates an eight-character filename that can be used by older programs. The eight-character filename is created from the first six nonspace characters in the long filename, with the addition of a tilde (~) and a number. For example, the filename Car Sales for 2004 would be converted to Carsal~1.

Most filenames have an extension. An **extension** (a set of no more than three characters at the end of a filename, separated from the filename by a period) is used by the operating system to identify and categorize the files by their file types. The characters also indicate the program in which the file was created. In the filename Car Sales for 2004.doc, for example, the file extension "doc" identifies the file as one created with Microsoft Word. You might also have a file called Car Sales for 2004.xls—the "xls" extension identifies the file as one created in Microsoft Excel, a spreadsheet program. When pronouncing filenames with extensions, say "dot" for the period, so that you pronounce the filename Resume.doc as "Resume dot doc."

You usually do not need to add an extension to a filename because the program that you use to create the file adds the file extension automatically. Also, Windows XP keeps track of extensions, but not all computers are set to display extensions. The steps in these tutorials refer to files using the filename without its extension. So if you see the filename Practice Text in the steps, but "Practice Text.doc" on your screen, both names refer to the same file. Also, you do not have to use lowercase and uppercase letters consistently when naming files. Usually the operating system doesn't distinguish between them. Be aware, however, that some programs are case-sensitive—that is, they check for case in filenames.

Now you can save the document you typed.

To start saving your document:

1. Click the **Save** button 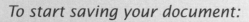 on the toolbar. The Save As dialog box opens, as shown in Figure 2-6.

Figure 2-6	SAVING A FILE

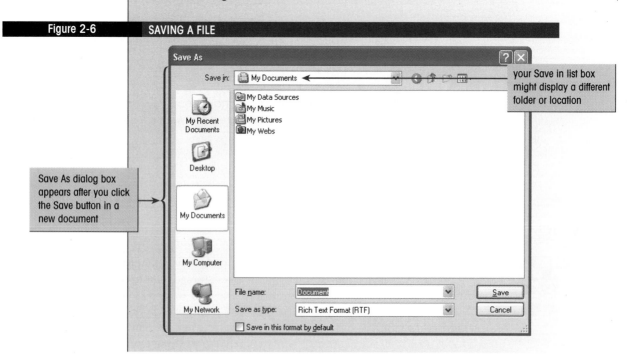

You use the Save As dialog box to specify where you want to save your file (on the hard disk or on a floppy disk, in a folder or not, and so on). Before going further with the process of saving a file, examine some of the features of the Save As dialog box so that you learn to save your files exactly where you want them.

Specifying the File Location

In the Save As dialog box, Windows XP provides the **Places Bar**, a list of important locations on your computer. When you click the different icons in the Places Bar, the contents of those locations will be displayed in the white area of the Save As dialog box. You can then save your document directly to those locations. Figure 2-7 identifies the icons in the Places Bar and gives their function.

Figure 2-7	ICONS IN THE PLACES BAR

ICON	DESCRIPTION
My Recent Documents	Displays a list of recently opened files, folders, and objects
Desktop	Displays a list of files, folders, and objects on the Windows XP desktop
My Documents	Displays a list of files, folders, and objects in the My Documents folder
My Computer	Displays a list of files, folders, and objects in the My Computer window
My Network Places	Displays a list of computers and folders available on the network

To see this in action, try displaying different locations in the Save As dialog box.

To use the Places Bar:

1. Click the **Desktop** icon in the Places Bar.

2. The Save As dialog box now displays the contents of the Windows XP desktop. See Figure 2-8.

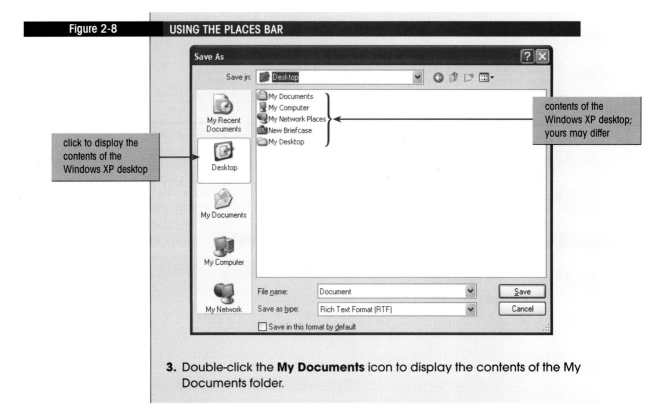

Figure 2-8   **USING THE PLACES BAR**

3. Double-click the **My Documents** icon to display the contents of the My Documents folder.

Once you've clicked an icon in the Places Bar, you can open any file displayed in that location, and you can save a file in that location. The Places Bar doesn't have an icon for every location on your computer, however. The Save in list box (located at the top of the dialog box) does. Use the Save in list box now to save your document on your floppy disk.

To use the Save in list box:

1. Click the **Save in** list arrow to display a list of drives.

2. Click **3½ Floppy (A:)**.

Now that you've specified where you want to save your file, you can specify a name and type for the file.

Specifying the File Name and Type

After choosing the location for your document, you have to specify the name of the file. You should also specify (or at least check) the file's format. A file's **format** determines what type of information you can place in the document, the document's appearance, and what kind of programs can work with the document. You can save a WordPad document in one of four file formats: Rich Text Format (RTF), Text, Text for MS-DOS, and Unicode Text. In addition, you can open a document in the Word for Windows 6.0 or Windows Write formats. The Word, Write, and RTF formats allow you to create documents with text that can use boldfaced or italicized fonts as well as documents containing graphic images and scanned photos. However, only word-processing programs like WordPad or Microsoft Word can work with those files. The four text formats allow only simple text with no graphics or special formatting, but such documents are readable by a wider range of programs. The default format for WordPad documents is RTF, but you can change that, as you'll see shortly.

Continue saving the document, using the name "Practice Text" and the file type Text Document.

To finish saving your document:

1. Select the text **Document** in the File name text box, and then type **Practice Text.** The new text replaces "Document."

2. Click the **Save as type** list arrow, and then click **Text Document** in the list. See Figure 2-9.

Figure 2-9	COMPLETED SAVE AS DIALOG BOX

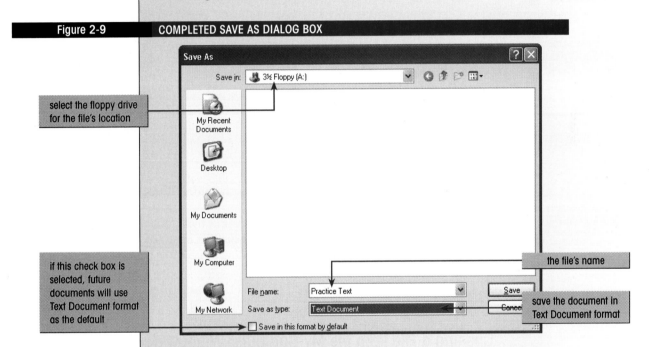

select the floppy drive for the file's location

the file's name

if this check box is selected, future documents will use Text Document format as the default

save the document in Text Document format

3. Click the **Save** button in the lower-right corner of the dialog box.

4. If you are asked whether you are sure that you want to save the document in this format, click the **Yes** button.

   Your file is saved on your Data Disk, and the document title, "Practice Text," appears in the WordPad title bar.

Note that after you save the file, the document appears a little different. What has changed? By saving the document in Text Document format rather than RTF, you've changed the format of the document slightly. One change is that the text is wrapped differently in Text Document format. A Text Document file does not wrap text when it reaches the right margin.

What if you try to close WordPad before you save your file? Windows XP will display a message—"Save changes to document?" If you answer "Yes," Windows XP will display the Save As dialog box so you can give the document a name. If you answer "No," Windows XP will close WordPad without saving the document. Any changes you made to the document will be lost. Unless you are absolutely sure you don't need to keep the work you just did, answer "Yes."

After you save a file, you can work on another document or close WordPad. Because you have already saved your Practice Text document, you'll continue this tutorial by closing WordPad.

To close WordPad:

1. Click the **Close** button ☒ to close the WordPad window.

Opening a File

Now that you have saved and closed the Practice Text file, suppose you now want to revise it. To revise a file you must first open it. When you open a file, its contents are copied into the computer's memory. If you revise the file, you need to save the changes before you close the file or close the program. If you close a revised file without saving your changes, you will lose them.

You can use one of several methods to open a file. If you have opened the file recently, you can select the file from the My Recent Documents list on the Start menu. The My Recent Documents list contains the 15 most recently opened documents. You can also locate and open a file using the My Computer window (or **Windows Explorer**, another Windows XP file management tool). Or you can start a program and then use the program's Open button (or Open command on the File menu) to locate and open the file. Each method has advantages and disadvantages.

Using one of the first two methods for opening the Practice Text file simply requires you to click the file in the My Recent Documents list or locate and select it from the My Computer window or Windows Explorer window. With these methods, the document, not the program, is central to the task; hence, these methods are sometimes referred to as **docucentric**. You only need to remember the name of your file—you do not need to remember which program you used to create it.

Opening a File from the My Computer Window

You can open a file by selecting it from the My Computer window or Windows Explorer window. Windows XP uses the file extension (whether it is displayed or not) to determine which program to start so you can work with the file. Windows XP starts the program and then opens the file. The advantage of this method is simplicity. The disadvantage is that Windows XP might not start the program you expect. For example, when you select Practice Text, you might expect Windows XP to start WordPad because you used WordPad to create it. Depending on the programs installed on your computer system, however, Windows XP might start Notepad or Microsoft Word instead. Notepad works with simple text files, such as those that have a .txt extension, and Word works with a wide range of documents that can include formatting, graphics, and other elements. Word files have a .doc extension. Using any word-processing program to open a text file is not usually a problem. Although the program might not be the one you expect, you can still use it to revise your file.

To open the Practice Text file by selecting it from My Computer:

1. Double-click the **My Computer** icon on the desktop to open the My Computer window.

2. Double-click the **3½ Floppy (A:)** icon in the My Computer window.

---

3. Double-click the **Practice Text** file icon. Windows XP starts Notepad and then opens the Practice Text file. You could edit the document at this point, but instead, you'll close all the windows on your desktop so you can try another method for opening files.

TROUBLE? If Windows XP starts Microsoft Word or another word-processing program instead of NotePad, continue with Step 4.

4. Close all open windows on the desktop.

Windows XP opened Practice Text in Notepad because you saved it as a text document—and Windows is usually setup to open text documents with Notepad. If you want to be sure to edit Practice Text in WordPad, first open WordPad and then use the Open button. You will try that next.

Opening a File from Within a Program

The advantage of opening a file from within a program is that you can specify the program you want to use to modify the file—WordPad, in this case. This method, however, involves more steps than the method you tried previously.

You can take advantage of the Places bar to reduce the number of steps it takes to open a file from within a program. Recall that the Places Bar contains the My Recent Documents icon, which when clicked, provides a list of recently opened files. One of the most recently opened files was the Practice Text file, so you should be able to open it using this method.

Open the Practice Text file using the Open button in WordPad.

To open a list of recent files and then save a WordPad document:

1. Start **WordPad** and maximize the WordPad window.

2. Click the **Open** button 📂 on the toolbar.

3. In the Open dialog box, click **My Recent Documents** in the Places bar.

The Practice Text file doesn't appear in the list. Why not? Look at the Files of Type list box. The selected entry is "Rich Text Format (rtf)". What this means is that the only files listed in the Open dialog box are those saved as Rich Text files—they all have an .rtf file extension. Limiting the types of files displayed frees you from having to deal with the clutter of unwanted or irrelevant files. The downside is that unless you're aware of how the Open dialog box will filter the list of files, you may mistakenly think that the file you're looking for doesn't exist. You can change how the Open dialog box filters this file list. Try this now by changing the filter to show only .txt documents.

To change the types of files displayed:

1. Click the **Files of type** list arrow. Note that WordPad can open files with a .doc or .wri extension, in addition to the file types it can save. Click **Text Documents (*.txt)**. The Practice Text file now appears in the list.

2. Click **Practice Text** in the list box. See Figure 2-10.

Figure 2-10	SELECTING THE FILE

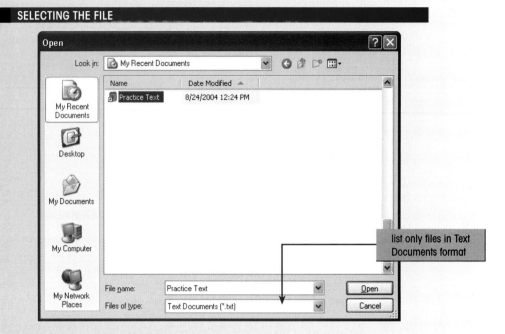

list only files in Text Documents format

3. Click the **Open** button. The document opens in the WordPad window. Note that you could also open the Practice Text file by double-clicking its name in the file list.

Saving the file as a Text Document did not preserve the word wrap. To restore word wrap, you can save the file in the Rich Text Format.

4. Click **File** on the menu bar, and then click **Save As**. You use the Save As command when you want to save the current file with a different name, file type, or location.

5. Click the **Save as type** list arrow, and then click **Rich Text Format (RTF)**.

6. Click the **Save** button. A message appears indicating that a file named Practice Text already exists in the selected location. You want to replace this file with one in the RTF format.

7. Click the **Yes** button. The word wrap in the Practice Text document is restored.

Now that you have opened and saved the Practice Text file as an RTF file, you can print it.

Printing a Document

Windows XP provides easy access to the printers connected to your computer. You can choose which printer to use, you can control how the document is printed, and you can control the order in which documents print. You also can preview your document before printing it to see how it will appear when it is printed.

Previewing Your Document Before Printing

Before you send a document to the printer, you should always preview it using Print Preview. **Print Preview** shows your document exactly as it will appear when printed on paper. You can check your page layout so you don't waste paper printing a document that is not quite the way you want it.

Preview and print the Practice Text document. Your instructor might supply you with additional instructions for printing in your lab.

To preview the Practice Text document:

1. Click the **Print Preview** button 🔍 on the WordPad toolbar.

TROUBLE? If an error message appears, printing capabilities might not be set up on your computer. Ask your instructor or technical support person for help, or skip this set of steps.

2. Look at your document in the Print Preview window. Before you print the document, you should make sure the font, margins, and other document features are the way you want them.

TROUBLE? If the document does not look the way you want it to, click the Close button, edit the document, and then click the Print Preview button again.

TROUBLE? If you can't read the document text on screen, click the Zoom In button as many times as necessary to read the text.

3. Click the **Close** button on the Print Preview toolbar to close Print Preview, and return to the document.

Now that you've verified that the document looks the way you want, you can print it.

Sending Your Document to the Printer

There are three ways to send your document to the printer. One way is to click the Print button 🖨 on your program's toolbar. This method will send the document directly to your printer—you do not need to take any further action. It's the quickest and easiest way to print a document, although it does not allow you to change settings such as margins and number of copies. What if you have access to more than one printer? In that case, Windows XP sends the document to the default printer, the one set up to handle your print tasks.

If you want to select a different printer or control how the printer prints your document, you can select the Print command from the File menu. Selecting the Print command opens the Print dialog box, allowing you to choose which printer to use and how that printer will print the document.

You can also print your document directly from the Print Preview window by clicking the Print button on the Print Preview toolbar. Clicking the Print button in Print Preview also opens the Print dialog box so you can verify or change settings.

Print the Practice Text document using the File menu.

To print the document using the Print command on the File menu:

1. Click **File** on the menu bar, and then click **Print**. The Print dialog box opens, as shown in Figure 2-11.

Figure 2-11	PRINTING A FILE

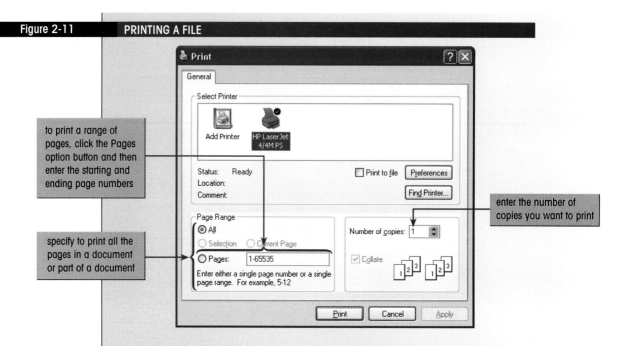

to print a range of pages, click the Pages option button and then enter the starting and ending page numbers

specify to print all the pages in a document or part of a document

enter the number of copies you want to print

2. Make sure your Print dialog box shows the Print range set to **All** and the number of copies set to **1**.

3. Click the **Print** button to print your document.

   TROUBLE? If your document does not print, make sure the printer is turned on and contains paper. If your document still doesn't print, ask your instructor or technical support person for help.

4. Close WordPad.

   TROUBLE? If you see the message "Save changes to Document?", click the No button.

You've now learned how to create, save, open, and print word-processed files—essential skills for students in distance learning courses that rely on word-processed reports transmitted across the Internet. Shannon assures you that the techniques you've just learned apply to most Windows XP programs.

Session 2.1 QUICK CHECK

1. A(n) _____ is a collection of data that has a name and is stored on a disk or other storage medium.

2. _____ erases the data on a disk and arranges the magnetic particles on the disk's surface so the disk can store data.

3. True or False: When you move the mouse pointer over a text entry area, the pointer's shape changes to an I-beam I.

4. What shows you where each character you type will appear?

5. _____ automatically moves text down to the beginning of the next line when you reach the right margin.

6. How do you select a block of text?

7. In the filename New Equipment.doc, doc is a(n) _____.

SESSION 2.2

In this session you will change the settings in the My Computer window to control its appearance and the appearance of desktop objects. You will use My Computer to manage the files on your Data Disk; view information about the files on your disk; organize the files into folders; and move, delete, copy, and rename files.

Using My Computer

The My Computer icon on the desktop represents your computer, its storage devices, printers, and other objects. The My Computer icon opens the My Computer window, which contains an icon for each of the storage devices on your computer, as shown in Figure 2-12. These icons appear in the right pane of the My Computer window. On most computer systems, the My Computer window also has a left pane, which shows icons and links to other resources. You'll learn more about the left pane shortly.

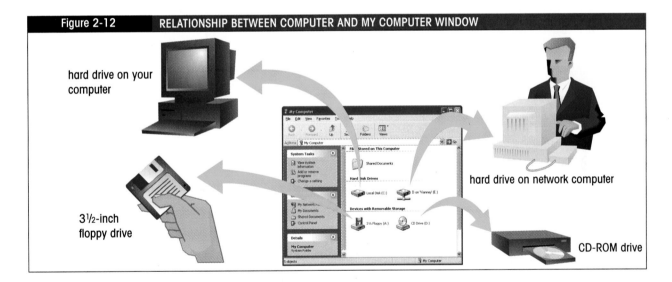

Figure 2-12   **RELATIONSHIP BETWEEN COMPUTER AND MY COMPUTER WINDOW**

hard drive on your computer

hard drive on network computer

3½-inch floppy drive

CD-ROM drive

Each storage device you have access to on your computer has a letter associated with it. The first floppy drive on a computer is usually designated as drive A. (If you add a second floppy drive, it is usually designated as drive B.) The first hard drive is usually designated drive C. (If you add additional hard drives, they are usually designated as D, E, and so on.) If you have a CD or DVD drive, it will usually have the next letter in the alphabetic sequence. If you have access to hard drives located on other computers in a network, those drives will sometimes (although not always) have letters associated with them as well. In the example shown in Figure 2-12, the network drive has the drive letter E.

You can use the My Computer window to keep track of where your files are stored and to organize your files. In this session, you will move and delete files on your Data Disk, which is assumed to be located in drive A. If you use your own computer at home or work, you will probably store your files on drive C instead of drive A. However, in a school lab environment you usually don't know which computer you will use, so you need to carry your files with you on a floppy disk that you can use in drive A on any computer. In this session, therefore, you will learn how to work with the files on drive A. Most of what you learn will also work on your home or work computer when you use drive C (or other drives).

Now you'll open the My Computer window.

To explore the contents of your Data Disk using the My Computer window:

1. Make sure your Data Disk is in the floppy drive. If necessary, remove the disk you formatted—the one that contains only the Practice Text file—and then insert your Data Disk in the floppy drive.

2. Open the My Computer window. See Figure 2-13.

Figure 2-13	MY COMPUTER WINDOW

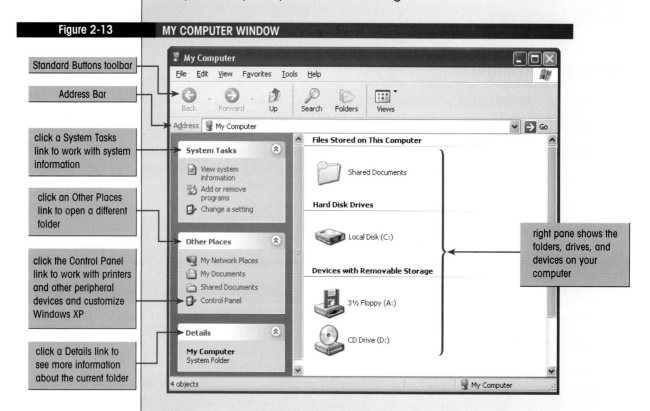

Standard Buttons toolbar

Address Bar

click a System Tasks link to work with system information

click an Other Places link to open a different folder

click the Control Panel link to work with printers and other peripheral devices and customize Windows XP

click a Details link to see more information about the current folder

right pane shows the folders, drives, and devices on your computer

Figure 2-14 identifies and describes the elements of the My Computer window.

Figure 2-14	ELEMENTS OF THE MY COMPUTER WINDOW

ELEMENT	DESCRIPTION
System Tasks	Click a System Tasks link to view system information, such as the capacity of your hard drive, add or remove programs, or change a system setting.
Other Places	Click an Other Places link to open the My Documents or Shared Documents folder or the Network Places or Control Panel Window.
Control Panel	Click this link to view or change your computer settings.
Details	If you are viewing the contents of a folder, click a Details link to see more information about the folder or device, such as its size and the date it was created on.
Right pane	Shows the folders, drives, and devices on your computer; double-click an icon to open the object.
Standard Buttons toolbar	Contains buttons for performing common tasks, such as navigating your computer or changing the icon view.
Address Bar	Shows the name and location of the current device or folder; you can enter a different location in the Address Bar to open a different folder or other object.

3. Double-click the **3½ Floppy (A:)** icon. A window opens showing the contents of drive A; maximize this window if necessary. See Figure 2-15.

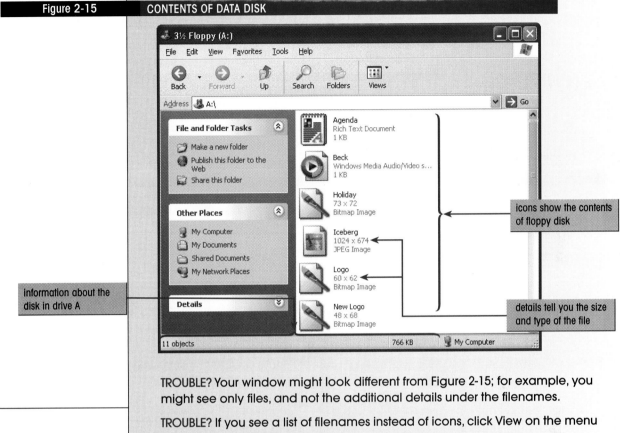

Figure 2-15   CONTENTS OF DATA DISK

TROUBLE? Your window might look different from Figure 2-15; for example, you might see only files, and not the additional details under the filenames.

TROUBLE? If you see a list of filenames instead of icons, click View on the menu bar, and then click Tiles.

TROUBLE? If you do not see the status bar, click New on the menu bar, and then click Status Bar.

Changing the Appearance of the My Computer Window

Windows XP offers several options that control how toolbars, icons, and buttons appear in the My Computer window. To make the My Computer window look the same as it does in the figures in this book, you need to ensure three things: that only the Standard and Address toolbars are visible; that files and other objects appear as Tiles, which displays files as large icons, and that the configuration of Windows XP uses the default setting. Setting your computer to match the figures makes it easier for you to follow the steps in these tutorials.

Controlling the Toolbar Display

The My Computer window, in addition to featuring a Standard toolbar, allows you to display the same toolbars that can appear on the Windows XP taskbar, such as the Address toolbar or the Links toolbar. You can use these toolbars to access the Web from the My Computer window. In this tutorial, however, you need to see only the Address and Standard Buttons toolbars.

To display only the Address and Standard Buttons toolbars:

1. Click **View** on the menu bar, and then point to **Toolbars**. The Standard Buttons and Address Bar commands on the Toolbars submenu should be checked, indicating that they are displayed in the My Computers window. The Links option should not be checked.

2. If the Standard Buttons or Address Bar commands *are not checked*, click the command to select it. Or if the Links option *is checked*, click it to deselect it. Note that you must display the Toolbars submenu to select or deselect each option.

3. If necessary, click **View** on the menu bar, and then point to **Toolbars** to verify that your Toolbars submenu and the toolbars displayed in the My Computer Window look like Figure 2-16.

Figure 2-16	CHECKING VIEW OPTIONS

TROUBLE? If the check marks on the Toolbars submenu are distributed differently than in Figure 2-16, repeat Steps 1 and 2 until the correct options are selected.

TROUBLE? If your toolbars' arrangement differs from that shown in Figure 2-16 (for example, both the Standard Buttons and Address toolbars are on the same line or the Standard Buttons toolbar is above the Address toolbar), you can easily rearrange them. To move a toolbar, first make sure it is unlocked. Click View on the menu bar, point to Toolbars, and then click Lock the Toolbar to uncheck this command. Then drag the vertical bar at the far left of the toolbar left, right, up, or down.

TROUBLE? If there are no labels included on the toolbar buttons, click View on the menu bar, point to Toolbars, click Customize, click the Text options list arrow in the Customize Toolbar dialog box, click Show text labels, and then click the Close button.

4. Press the **Esc** key to close the Toolbars menu.

Changing the Icon Display

Windows XP provides five ways to view the contents of a disk—Thumbnails, Tiles, Icons, List, and Details. Figure 2-17 shows examples of these five styles.

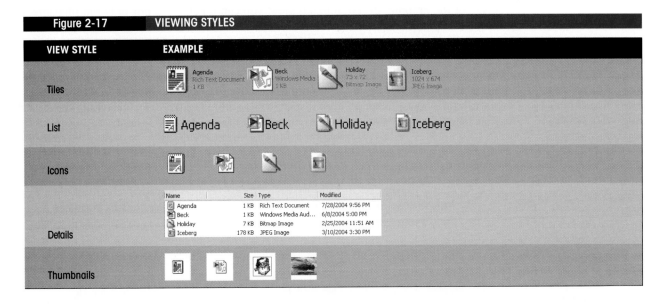

| Figure 2-17 | VIEWING STYLES |

The default view, **Tiles view**, displays a large icon, title, file type, and file size for each file. The icon provides a visual cue to the type of file, as shown in Figure 2-18. You also can find this same information with the smaller icons displayed in the **Icons** and **List views**, but in less screen space. In Icons and List views, you can see more files and folders at one time, which is helpful when you have many files in one location.

| Figure 2-18 | TYPICAL ICONS IN WINDOWS XP |

FILE AND FOLDER ICONS

Text documents that you can open using the Notepad accessory are represented by notepad icons.

Graphic image documents that you can open using the Paint accessory are represented by drawing instruments.

Word-processed documents that you can open using the WordPad accessory are represented by a formatted notepad icon, unless your computer designates a different word-processing program to open files created with WordPad.

Word-processed documents that you can open using a program such as Microsoft Word are represented by formatted document icons.

Files created by programs that Windows does not recognize are represented by the Windows logo.

A folder icon represents folders.

Certain folders created by Windows XP have a special icon design related to the folder's purpose.

PROGRAM ICONS

Icons for programs usually depict an object related to the function of the program. For example, an icon that looks like a calculator represents the Calculator accessory.

Non-Windows programs are represented by the icon of a blank window.

All of the three icon views (Tiles, Icons, and List) help you quickly identify a file and its type, but what if you want more information about a set of files? **Details view** shows more information than the other three views. Details view shows the file icon, filename, file size, program used to create the file, and the date and time the file was created or last modified.

If you have graphic files, you can use **Thumbnails view**, which displays a small preview image of the graphic. In Thumbnails view, you can quickly see not only the filename, but also which picture or drawing the file contains. Thumbnails view is great for browsing a large collection of graphic files, but switching to this view can be time-consuming because Windows XP must first create all the preview images.

To practice switching from one view to another, start by displaying the contents of drive A in Details view. So far, you've used the View menu to change the window view. Now you can use the Views button, which displays the same commands for changing views as the View menu.

To view a detailed list of files:

1. Click the **Views** button 🖽 ˇ on the Standard Buttons toolbar, and then click **Details** to display details for the files on your disk. See Figure 2-19. Your files might be listed in a different order.

Figure 2-19 | DETAILS VIEW

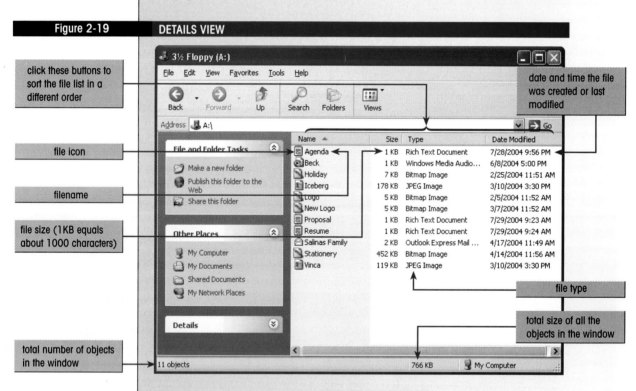

2. Look at the file sizes. Which files are the largest?

3. Look at the Type column. Which file is an Outlook Express Mail Message?

One of the advantages of Details view is that you can sort the file list by filename, size, type, or date. This helps if you're working with a large file list and you're trying to find a specific file.

To sort the file list by type:

1. Click the **Type** button at the top of the list of files. The files are now sorted in alphabetical order by type, starting with the Bitmap Image files and ending with the Windows XP Audio/Visual Media file.

   If you were looking for all the .rtf files (those created with WordPad, for example), sorting by type would be useful because the .rtf files would all be grouped together under "R" for Rich Text Format.

2. Click the **Type** button again. The sort order is reversed, with the Windows XP Audio/Visual Media file now at the top of the list.

3. Click the **Name** button at the top of the file list. The files are now sorted in alphabetical order by filename.

Now that you have looked at the file details, you can switch back to Tiles view.

To switch to Tiles view:

1. Click the **Views** button ▦ ˙ on the Standard Buttons toolbar, and then click **Tiles** to return to the Tiles view.

Restoring the My Computer Default Settings

Windows XP provides other options for working with your files and windows. These options fall into two general categories: Classic style and Web style. **Classic style** lets you interact with windows and files using techniques from earlier versions of the Windows operating system. **Web style** lets you work with windows and files in the same way you work with Web pages on the World Wide Web. For example, to open a file in Classic style, you can double-click the file icon or the filename, or you can click the file icon or filename once and press the Enter key. To open a file in Web style, you would point to a file icon until the pointer changed to 🖑, and then you would click the file icon once. The filenames would also appear underlined, indicating you can click once to open them. Underlined text is usually called a **hyperlink** or just **link**. You can also create your own style, choosing elements of both the Classic and Web styles, and add customized features of your own.

Try switching to the Web style to see how it works in the My Computer window. Then, to maintain consistency and make sure your screens match the ones in this tutorial, you'll return to the default style—the one Windows XP uses when it's initially installed. No matter what changes you make to the setup of Windows XP, you can always revert to the default style.

To switch to the Web style and back to the default style:

1. Click **Tools** on the menu bar, and then click **Folder Options**.

2. If necessary, click the **General** tab in the Folder Options dialog box. The General sheet includes options for working with files and windows.

3. In the Click items as follows section, click the **Single-click to open an item (point to select)** option button. When you select this option button, the Underline icon titles consistent with my browser option button is also selected. This means that filenames will always be underlined to indicate that you can click to open them.

4. Click the **OK** button. The filenames in the My Computer window are underlined as hyperlinks.

5. In the My Computer window, point to the **Agenda** icon. The icon is highlighted, indicating it is selected, and after a few moments, a ScreenTip appears. See Figure 2-20.

Figure 2-20 | MY COMPUTER WINDOW IN WEB STYLE

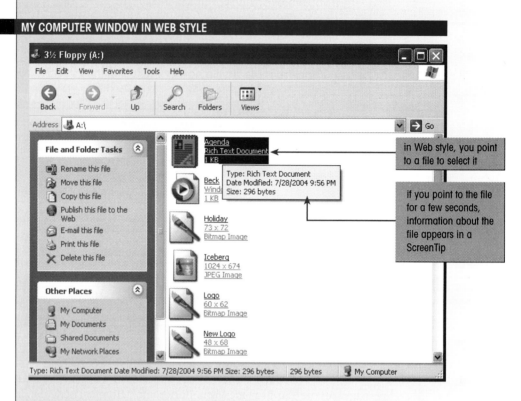

In Web style, when you move the pointer over an icon or underlined text, it appears as a hand ☝, indicating the icon or text is a hyperlink. In Classic style, when you point to an icon or filename, the pointer is a selection arrow ⌖.

6. To restore the default style, click **Tools** on the menu bar, and then click **Folder Options**.

7. Click the **Restore Defaults** button in the Folder Options dialog box.

8. Click the **View** tab. The View tab includes options that control the appearance of files and other objects. You need to make sure these options are set to their default settings as well.

9. Click the **Restore Defaults** button.

10. Click the **OK** button to close the Folder Options dialog box.

Working with Folders and Directories

Up to now, you've done a little work with files and windows, but before going further, you should look at some of the terminology used to describe these tasks. Any location where you can store files on a computer is called a **directory**. The main directory of a disk is sometimes called the **root directory**, or the **top-level directory**. All of the files on your Data Disk are currently in the root directory of your floppy disk.

If too many files are stored in a directory, the directory list becomes very long and difficult to manage. You can divide a directory into **subdirectories**, also called **folders**. The number of files for each folder then becomes much fewer and easier to manage. A folder within a folder is called a **subfolder**. The folder that contains another folder is called the **parent folder**.

Windows XP arranges all of these objects—root directory, folders, subfolders, and files—in a **hierarchy**. The hierarchy begins with your desktop and extends down to each subfolder. Figure 2-21 shows part of a typical hierarchy of Windows XP objects.

Figure 2-21	PART OF A TYPICAL HIERARCHY OF WINDOWS XP OBJECTS

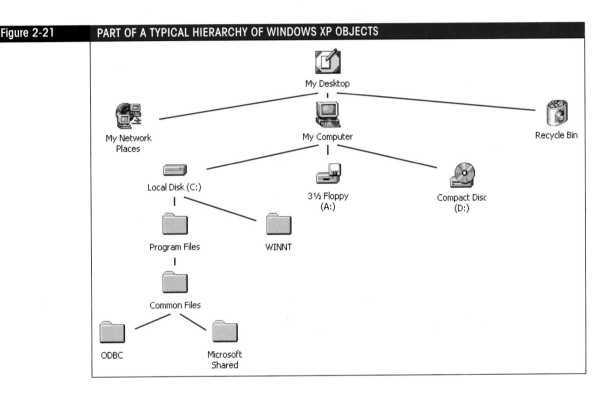

Creating a Folder

You've already seen folder icons in the windows you've opened. Now you'll create your own folder called Practice to hold your documents. This time, you can work in Icons view so you can see all the files on the Data Disk.

To create a Practice folder:

1. Click the **Views** button 🔲 ⁀ on the Standard Buttons toolbar, and then click **Icons**.

2. Click **File** on the menu bar, and then point to **New** to display the submenu.

3. Click **Folder**. A folder icon with the label "New Folder" appears in the My Computer window.

4. Type **Practice** as the name of the folder.

   TROUBLE? If nothing happens when you type the folder name, it's possible that the folder name is no longer selected. Right-click the new folder, click Rename on the shortcut menu, and then repeat Step 4.

5. Press the **Enter** key. The new folder is now named "Practice" and is the selected item on your Data Disk.

6. Click a blank area next to the Practice folder to deselect it.

Navigating Through the Windows XP Hierarchy

Now that you've created a folder, how do you move into it? You've learned that to view the contents of a file, you open it. To move into a folder, you open it in the same way.

To view the contents of the Practice folder:

1. Double-click the **Practice** folder. The Practice folder opens.

Because the folder doesn't contain any files, there's nothing listed in the right pane of the My Computer window. You'll change that shortly.

You've learned that to navigate through your computer, you open My Computer and then click the icons representing the objects you want to explore, such as folders and files. But what if you want to move back to the root directory? The Standard Buttons toolbar, which stays the same regardless of which folder or object is open, includes buttons that help you navigate the hierarchy of drives, directories, folders, subfolders, and other objects in your computer. Figure 2-22 summarizes the navigation buttons on the Standard Buttons toolbar.

Figure 2-22		NAVIGATION BUTTONS
BUTTON	**ICON**	**DESCRIPTION**
Back	⬅	Returns you to the folder, drive, directory, or object you were most recently viewing. The button is active only when you have viewed more than one window in the current session.
Forward	➡	Reverses the effect of the Back button.
Up	⤴	Moves you up one level in the hierarchy of directories, drives, folders, and other objects on your computer.

You can return to your floppy's root directory by using the Back or Up buttons. Try both of these techniques now.

To move up to the root directory:

1. Click the **Back** button ⬅ on the Standard Buttons toolbar. Windows XP opens the previous window, in this case, the root directory of your Data Disk.

2. Click the **Forward** button ➡ on the Standard Buttons toolbar. The Forward button reverses the effect of the Back button and takes you to the Practice folder.

3. Click the **Up** button ⤴ on the Standard Buttons toolbar. You move up one level in the hierarchy of Windows XP objects, to the root directory of the Data Disk.

Another way of moving around in the Windows XP hierarchy is through the Address Bar. By clicking the Address Bar list arrow, you can view a list of the objects in the top part of the Windows XP hierarchy, as illustrated in Figure 2-23. This gives you a quick way of moving to the top without navigating through the intermediate levels.

Figure 2-23	A HIERARCHY OF OBJECTS IN THE ADDRESS LIST BOX

Now that you know how to move around your computer's hierarchy, you can practice manipulating files. The more organized the hierarchy of your computer, the easier it is to find the files you need.

Working with Files

Using Files

As you've seen, the Practice folder doesn't contain any files. To add files to a folder or drive, you can move a file from one place to another or copy a file so you have duplicates in two locations. After you copy a file, you might want to rename it—that way, you won't confuse it with the original file. If you no longer use a file, you can delete it from your disk. You should periodically delete files you no longer need, so your folders and disks don't get too full and slow the performance of your system.

My Computer simplifies these tasks because you can move, copy, rename, and delete files using the My Computer window. Next, you will use My Computer to place a file from the root directory in the Practice folder.

Moving and Copying a File

If you want to place a file in a folder from another location, you can either move the file or copy it. **Moving** a file removes it from its current location and places it in a new location you specify. **Copying** leaves the file in its current location and places a copy in the new location. Windows XP provides several techniques for moving and copying files. One way is to make sure that both the current and the new location are visible on your screen and then hold down the right mouse button and drag the file from the old location to the new location. A menu appears, including options to move or copy the selected file to the new location. The advantage to this technique is that it is clear whether you are moving or copying a file. Try this technique now by moving the Logo file to the Practice folder.

To move the Logo file to the Practice folder:

1. Point to the **Logo** file in the root directory of your Data Disk, and then press and hold the *right* mouse button.

2. With the right mouse button still pressed down, drag the **Logo** file to the Practice folder. When the Practice folder icon is highlighted, release the button. A shortcut menu appears, as shown in Figure 2-24.

| Figure 2-24 | MOVING A FILE |

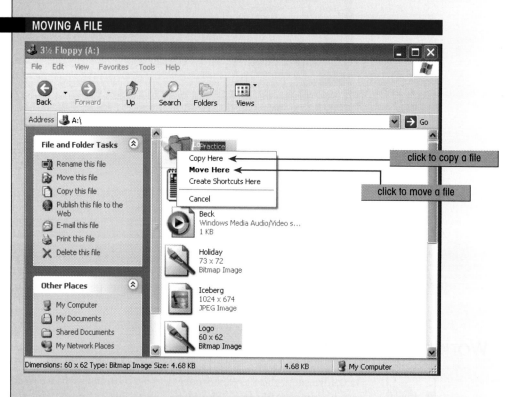

3. Click **Move Here** on the shortcut menu with the left mouse button. The Logo file is removed from the window showing the files in the root directory.

TROUBLE? If you release the mouse button by mistake before dragging the Logo file to the Practice folder, the Logo shortcut menu opens. Press the Esc key, and then repeat Steps 1 through 3.

4. Double-click the **Practice** folder. The Logo file now appears in the Practice folder.

You can also copy a file from one folder to another, or from one disk to another. When you copy a file, you create an exact duplicate of a file in whatever disk or folder you specify. To copy a file from one folder to another on your floppy disk, you use the same procedure as for moving a file, except that you select Copy Here on the shortcut menu. Try copying the Agenda file into the Practice folder.

To copy the Agenda file into the Practice folder:

1. Click the **Up** button 🔼 on the Standard Buttons toolbar. The root directory of your Data Disk is displayed.

2. Using the right mouse button, drag the **Agenda** file into the Practice folder.

---

3. Using the left mouse button, click **Copy Here** on the shortcut menu. Notice this time the file is not removed from the root directory because you copied the file.

4. Double-click the **Practice** folder. A copy of the Agenda file now appears in the Practice folder.

Note that the Move Here command was also on the shortcut menu. In fact, the command was in boldface, indicating that it is the default command whenever you drag a document from one location to another on the same drive. This means that if you were to drag a file from one location to another on the same drive using the left mouse button (instead of the right), the file would be moved and not copied.

Renaming a File

Sometimes you decide to give a file a different name to clarify the file's contents. You can easily rename a file by using the Rename command on the file's shortcut menu.

Practice this technique by renaming the Agenda file to give it a more descriptive filename.

To rename the Agenda file:

1. Make sure the right pane is set to Tiles view. If necessary, click the **Views** button on the Standard Buttons toolbar, and then click **Tiles**.

2. Right-click the **Agenda** icon.

3. Click **Rename** on the shortcut menu. The filename is highlighted and a box appears around it.

4. Type **Practice Agenda** and press the **Enter** key. The file now appears with the new name.

TROUBLE? If you make a mistake while typing and you haven't pressed the Enter key yet, you can press the Backspace key until you delete the mistake, and then complete Step 3. If you've already pressed the Enter key, repeat Steps 1 through 3 to rename the file again.

Deleting a File or Folder

You should periodically delete files you no longer need so that your folders and disks don't get cluttered. In My Computer, you delete a file or folder by deleting its icon. Be careful when you delete a folder, because you also delete all the files it contains! When you delete a file from a hard drive on your computer, the filename is deleted from the directory but the file contents are held in the Recycle Bin. The **Recycle Bin** is an area on your hard drive that holds deleted files until you remove them permanently; an icon on the desktop allows you easy access to the Recycle Bin. If you change your mind and want to retrieve a file deleted from your hard drive, you can recover it by using the Recycle Bin. However, after you empty the Recycle Bin, you can no longer recover the files that were in it.

When you delete a file from a floppy disk or another disk on your network, it does not go into the Recycle Bin. Instead, it is deleted as soon as its icon disappears—and you can't recover it.

Try deleting the Practice Agenda file from your Data Disk. Because this file is on the floppy disk and not on the hard disk, it will not go into the Recycle Bin. If you change your mind, you won't be able to recover it.

To delete the Practice Agenda file:

1. Right-click the **Practice Agenda** file icon.

2. Click **Delete** on the shortcut menu.

A message box appears, Windows XP asking if you're sure you want to delete this file.

3. Click the **Yes** button.

4. Click the **Close** button ☒ to close the My Computer window.

Another way of deleting a file is to drag its icon to the Recycle Bin on the desktop. Be aware that if you're dragging a file from your floppy disk or network drive, the file will *not* be placed in the Recycle Bin—it will be permanently deleted.

Other Copying and Moving Techniques

As you become more familiar with Windows XP, you will probably settle on the copying and moving technique you like best. Figure 2-25 describes some of the other ways of moving and copying files.

Figure 2-25	METHODS FOR MOVING AND COPYING FILES	
METHOD	**TO MOVE**	**TO COPY**
Cut, copy and paste	Select the file icon. Click Edit on the menu bar, and then click Cut. Move to the new location. Click Edit and then click Paste.	Select the file icon. Click Edit on the menu bar, and then click Copy. Move to the new location. Click Edit and then click Paste.
Drag and drop	Click the file icon. Drag and drop the icon to the new location.	Click the file icon. Hold down the Ctrl key, and drag and drop the icon to the new location.
Right-click, drag and drop	With the right mouse button pressed down, drag the file icon to the new location. Release the mouse button, and click Move Here on the shortcut menu.	With the right mouse button pressed down, drag the file icon to the new location. Release the mouse button, and click Copy Here on the shortcut menu.
Move to folder and copy to folder	Click the file icon. Click Edit on the menu bar, and then click Move to Folder. Select the new location in the Browse for Folder dialog box.	Click the file icon. Click Edit on the menu bar, and then click Copy to Folder. Select the new location in the Browse for Folder dialog box.

The techniques shown in Figure 2-25 are primarily for document (data) files. Because a program might not work correctly if moved to a new location, the techniques for moving program files are slightly different. See the Windows XP online Help for more information on moving or copying a program file.

Copying an Entire Floppy Disk

You can have trouble accessing the data on your floppy disk if the disk is damaged, is exposed to magnetic fields, or picks up a computer virus. To avoid losing all your data, you should always make a copy of your floppy disk.

If you wanted to make a copy of a videotape, your VCR would need two tape drives. You might wonder, therefore, how your computer can make a copy of your disk if you have only one floppy disk drive. Figure 2-26 illustrates how the computer uses only one disk drive to make a copy of a disk.

Figure 2-26 | **USING ONE DISK DRIVE TO COPY A DISK**

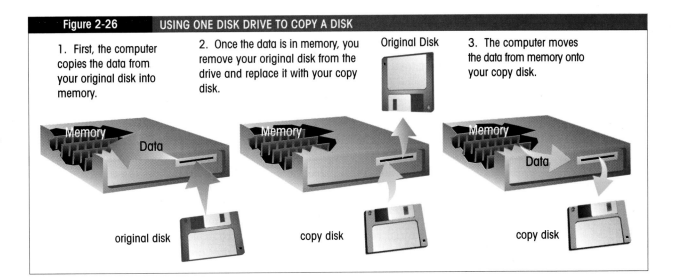

1. First, the computer copies the data from your original disk into memory.

2. Once the data is in memory, you remove your original disk from the drive and replace it with your copy disk.

Original Disk

3. The computer moves the data from memory onto your copy disk.

original disk

copy disk

copy disk

REFERENCE   WINDOW   **RW**

<u>Copying a Disk</u>
- Insert the disk you want to copy in drive A.
- In My Computer, right-click the 3½ Floppy (A:) icon, and then click Copy Disk.
- Click Start to begin the copy process.
- When prompted, remove the disk you want to copy, place your second disk in drive A, and then click OK.

If you have an extra floppy disk, you can make a copy of your Data Disk now. Make sure you copy the disk regularly so that as you work through the tutorials in the book the disk stays updated.

To copy your Data Disk:

1. Write your name and "Windows XP Disk 1 Data Disk Copy" on the label of a blank, formatted disk.

   TROUBLE? If you aren't sure the disk is blank, place it in the disk drive and open the 3½ Floppy (A:) window to view its contents. If the disk contains files you need, get a different disk. If it contains files you don't need, you could format the disk now, using the steps you learned at the beginning of this tutorial.

2. Make sure your original Data Disk is in drive A, and then open and maximize the My Computer window.

3. Right-click the 3½ **Floppy (A:)** icon, and then click **Copy Disk**. The Copy Disk dialog box opens.

4. Click the **Start** button to begin the copy process.

5. When the message "Insert the disk you want to copy from (source disk)" appears, click **OK**. Windows XP reads the disk in drive A and stores its contents in memory.

6. Click the **OK** button. When the copy is completed, you will see the message "Copy completed successfully."

7. Click the **Close** button to close the Copy Disk dialog box.

8. Close the My Computer window, and then remove your disk from the drive.

As you finish copying your disk, Shannon emphasizes the importance of making copies of your files frequently, so you won't risk losing important documents for your distance learning course. If your original Data Disk were damaged, you could use the copy you just made to access the files.

Keeping copies of your files is so important that Windows XP includes with it a program called **Backup** that automates the process of duplicating and storing data. In the Projects at the end of the tutorial you'll have an opportunity to explore the difference between what you just did in copying a disk and the way in which a program such as the Windows XP Backup program helps you safeguard data.

Session 2.2 QUICK CHECK

1. If you want to find out about the storage devices and printers connected to your computer, what Windows XP window can you open?

2. If you have only one floppy disk drive on your computer, the letter _____ usually identifies it.

3. The letter C typically designates the _____ drive of a computer.

4. What information does Details view supply about a list of folders and files?

5. The main directory of a disk is referred to as the _____ directory.

6. True or False: You can divide a directory into folders.

7. If you have one floppy disk drive and two floppy disks, can you copy the files on one floppy disk to the other?

REVIEW ASSIGNMENTS

1. **Opening, Editing, and Printing a Document** In this tutorial you learned how to create a document using WordPad. You also learned how to save, open, and print a document. Practice these skills by opening the document called **Resume** on your Data Disk. This document is a resume for Jamie Woods. Make the changes shown in Figure 2-27, and then save the document in the Practice folder with the name **Woods Resume** using the Save As command. After you save your revisions, preview and then print the document. Close WordPad.

Figure 2-27

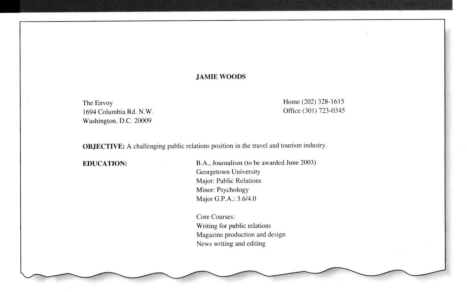

2. **Creating, Saving, and Printing a Letter** Use WordPad to write a one-page letter to a relative or a friend. Save the document in the Practice folder on your Data Disk with the name **Letter**. Use the Print Preview feature to look at the format of your finished letter, then print it, and be sure to sign it. Close WordPad.

3. **Managing Files and Folders** Using the copy of the disk you made at the end of the tutorial, complete Steps a through f below to practice your file-management skills. Then answer Questions 1 through 5 below.

     a. Create a folder called "Documents" on the copy of your Data Disk.

     b. Move the files Agenda, Proposal, and Resume to the Documents folder.

     c. Create a folder called "Park Project."

     d. Move the files New Logo, Stationery, and Vinca to the Park Project folder.

     e. Delete the file called "Logo."

     f. Switch to Details view, and write out your answers to Questions 1 through 5:

         1. What is the largest file in the Park Project folder?

         2. What is the newest file in the Documents folder?

         3. How many files are in the root directory of your Data Disk? (Don't count folders.)

         4. How are the Salinas Family and Iceberg icons different? Judging from the appearance of the icons, what would you guess these two files contain?

         5. Which file in the root directory has the most recent date?

4. **More Practice with Files and Folders** For this assignment, you need a third blank disk. Complete parts a through g below to practice your file-management skills.

     a. Write "Windows XP Tutorial 2 Assignment 4" on the label of the blank disk, and then format the disk if necessary.

     b. Create another copy of your original Data Disk, using the Assignment 4 disk. Refer to the section "Copying an Entire Floppy Disk" in Session 2.2.

     c. Create three folders on the Assignment 4 Data Disk you just created: Documents, Meetings, and Graphics.

     d. Move the files Iceberg, Holiday, Logo, and New Logo to the Graphics folder.

     e. Move the files Resume and Salinas Family to the Documents folder.

     f. Move Agenda and Stationery to the Meetings folder.

     g. Switch to Details view, and write out your answers to Questions 1 through 5.

         1. What is the largest file in the Graphics folder?

         2. How many documents created with a word-processing program are in the root directory? (*Hint*: These documents will appear with the WordPad, Microsoft Word, or some other word-processing icon, depending on what software you have installed.)

         3. What is the newest file or files in the root directory? (Don't include folders.)

         4. How many files in all folders are 5KB in size?

         5. How many files in the root directory are JPEG images? (*Hint*: Look in the Type column to identify JPEG images.)

         6. Do all the files in the Graphics folder have the same icon? What type are they?

Explore

5. **Searching for a File** Windows XP Help includes topics that explain how to search for files on a disk without looking through all the folders. Start Windows Help and use one of the following methods to locate topics on searching for files.

   ■ On the Home page, click the Windows basics link. On the Windows basics page, click the Searching for information link, and then click the Search for a file or folder topic. In the article, click the Related Topics link, and then click Search for a file or folder.

   ■ On the Index page, type "files and folders" (no quotation marks) in the Type in the keyword to find text box and then click the Display button. In the list of entries for "files and folders," double-click "searching for." In the Topics found dialog box, double-click "To search for a file or folder."

   ■ In the Search box, type "searching for files and folders" and then press the Enter key. Click the Search for a file or folder link.

   Read the topic and click the Related Topics link at the end of the topic, if necessary, to answer Questions a through c:

   a. How do you display the Search window?
   b. Do you need to type the entire filename in the Search window to find the file?
   c. What are three file characteristics you can use as Search options?

6. **Help with Managing Files and Folders** In Tutorial 2 you learned how to work with Windows XP files and folders. Use the Index page in Windows XP Help and Support to find an overview of files and folders. Use the Related Topics link to find two procedures for managing files and folders that were not covered in the tutorial. Write out the procedures in your own words, and include the title of the Help page that contains the information.

Explore

7. **Formatting Text** You can use a word processor such as WordPad to **format** text, that is, to change its appearance by using bold, italic, and different fonts, and by applying other features. Using WordPad, type the title and words of one of your favorite songs, and then save the document on your Data Disk with the name **Song**. (Make sure to use your original Data Disk.)

   a. Select the title of the song, click the Center button ▤ on the toolbar, click the Bold button **B**, and then click the Italic button *I*.
   b. Click the list arrow for the Font button on the toolbar, and then select a different font. Repeat this step several times with different fonts until you locate a font that is appropriate for the song.
   c. Experiment with formatting options until you find a look you like for your document. Save and print the final version.

PROJECTS

1. Formatting a floppy disk removes all the data on a disk. Answer the following questions:

    a. What other method did you learn in this tutorial to remove data from a disk?

    b. If you wanted to remove all data from a disk, which method would you use? Why?

    c. What method would you use if you wanted to remove only one file? Why?

2. A friend who is new to computers is trying to learn how to enter text into WordPad. She has just finished typing her first paragraph when she notices a mistake in the first sentence. She can't remember how to fix a mistake, so she asks you for help. Write the set of steps that she should follow.

3. Computer users usually develop habits about how they access their files and programs. Take a minute to practice methods of opening a file, and then evaluate which method you would be most likely to use and why.

    a. Using WordPad, create a document containing the words to a favorite poem, and save it on your Data Disk with the name **Poem**.

    b. Close WordPad and return to the desktop.

    c. Open the document using a *docucentric* approach.

    d. After a successful completion of part c, close the program and reopen the same document using another approach.

    e. Write the steps that you used to complete parts c and d of this assignment. Then write a paragraph discussing which approach is most convenient when you are starting from the desktop, and indicate what habits you would develop if you owned your own computer and used it regularly.

Explore

4. The My Computer window gives you access to the objects on your computer. In this tutorial you used My Computer to access your floppy drive so you could view the contents of your Data Disk. The My Computer window gives you access to other objects, too. Open My Computer and write a list of the objects you see, including folders. Then double-click each icon and write a two-sentence description of the contents of each window that opens.

Explore

5. In this tutorial you learned how to copy a disk to protect yourself in the event of data loss. If you had your own computer with a 40GB hard drive that was being used to capacity, it would take many 1.44MB floppy disks to copy the contents of the entire hard drive. Is copying a reasonable method to use for protecting the data on your hard disk? Why, or why not?

   a. Windows XP includes an accessory called Backup that helps you safeguard your data. Backup doesn't just copy the data, it organizes the data so that it takes up much less space than if you simply copied it. This program might not be installed on your computer, but if it is, try starting it (click the Start button, point to all Programs, point to Accessories, point to System Tools, and then click Backup) and opening the Help files to learn what you can about how it functions. If it is not installed, continue with part b.

   b. Look up the topic of backups in a computer concepts textbook or in computer trade magazines. You could also interview experienced computer owners to find out which method they use to protect their data. When you have finished researching the concept of the backup, write a single-page essay that explains the difference between copying and backing up files, and that evaluates which method is preferable for backing up large amounts of data, and why.

LAB ASSIGNMENTS

Using Files In this Lab you manipulate a simulated computer to view what happens in memory and on disk when you create, save, open, revise, and delete files. Understanding what goes on "inside the box" will help you quickly grasp how to perform basic file operations with most application software. See the Read This Before You Begin page for instructions on starting the Using Files Course Lab.

1. Click the Steps button to learn how to use the simulated computer to view the contents of the memory and disk when you perform basic file operations. As you proceed through the Steps, answer all of the Quick Check questions that appear. After you complete the Steps, you will see a Quick Check Summary Report. Follow the instructions on the screen to print this report.

2. Click the Explore button and use the simulated computer to perform the following tasks:
   a. Create a document containing your name and the city in which you were born. Save this document as NAME.
   b. Create another document containing two of your favorite foods. Save this document as FOODS.
   c. Create another file containing your two favorite classes. Call this file CLASSES.
   d. Open the FOOD file and add another one of your favorite foods. Save this file without changing its name.
   e. Open the NAME file. Change this document so it contains your name and the name of your school. Save this as a new document called SCHOOL.
   f. Write down how many files are on the simulated disk and the exact contents of each file.
   g. Delete all the files.

3. In Explore, use the simulated computer to perform the following tasks.
   a. Create a file called MUSIC that contains the name of your favorite CD.
   b. Create another document that contains eight numbers, and call this file LOTTERY.
   c. You didn't win the lottery this week. Revise the contents of the LOTTERY file but save the revision as LOTTERY2.
   d. Revise the MUSIC file so it also contains the name of your favorite musician or composer, and save this file as MUSIC2.
   e. Delete the MUSIC file.
   f. Write down how many files are on the simulated disk and the exact contents of each file.

QUICK CHECK ANSWERS

Session 2.1

1. file
2. Formatting
3. True
4. insertion point
5. word wrap
6. Move the I-beam pointer to the left of the first word you want to select, and then drag the I-beam pointer over the text to the end of the last word you want to select.
7. file extension

Session 2.2

1. My Computer
2. A
3. hard
4. filename, size, type, and date modified
5. root or top-level
6. True
7. yes

TASK	PAGE #	RECOMMENDED METHOD
Character, insert	WIN 2.07	Click where you want to insert the character, type the character
Desktop, access	WIN 1.14	Click ⬜ on the Quick Launch toolbar
Disk, format	WIN 2.02	Right-click the 3½ Floppy icon in My Computer, click Format on the shortcut menu, click Start
File, copy	WIN 2.28	Use the right mouse button to drag the file you want to copy, release the mouse button, click Copy Here on the shortcut menu
File, delete	WIN 2.30	Right-click the file you want to delete, click Delete on the shortcut menu
File, move	WIN 2.28	Use the right mouse button to drag the file you want to copy, release the mouse button, click Move Here on the shortcut menu
File, open from My Computer	WIN 2.12	Open My Computer, open the Window containing the file, double-click the file
File, open from within a program	WIN 2.13	Start the program, click ⬜, select the file in the Open dialog box, click Open
File, preview before printing	WIN 2.15	Click ⬜
File, print	WIN 2.15	Click ⬜
File, rename	WIN 2.29	Right-click the file, click Rename on shortcut menu, type new filename, press Enter
File, save	WIN 2.08	Click ⬜
Files, view as large icons	WIN 2.21	Click the Views button, click Tiles
Files, view as small icons	WIN 2.21	Click the Views button, click Icons
Files, view details	WIN 2.22	Click the Views button, click Details
Files, view in list	WIN 2.21	Click the Views button, click List
Files, view thumbnails	WIN 2.21	Click the Views button, click Thumbnails
Floppy disk, copy	WIN 2.31	Right-click the 3½" Floppy icon in My Computer, click Copy Disk on the shortcut menu, click Start, insert the disk you want to copy from (sourcedisk), then click OK
Folder, create	WIN 2.25	Click File, point to New, click Folder, type a folder name, press Enter
Folder hierarchy, move back in the	WIN 2.26	Click ⬜
Folder hierarchy, move forward in the	WIN 2.26	Click ⬜
Folder hierarchy, move up	WIN 2.26	Click ⬜
Folder options, restore default settings	WIN 2.23	Click Tools, click Folder Options, click the General tab, click Restore Defaults, (or click the View tab and click Restore Defaults), click OK
Help, display topic from the Home page	WIN 1.30	In Help and Sudpport, click Home in the navigation bar
Help, display topic from the Index page	WIN 1.31	In Help, click Index in the navigation bar, scroll to locate a topic or type a keyword, click the topic, click Display

TASK REFERENCE

TASK	PAGE #	RECOMMENDED METHOD
Help, find topic	WIN 1.33	In Help, click in the Search box, type word or phrase, click ➡
Help, start	WIN 1.29	Click **start**, click Help and Support
Insertion point, move	WIN 2.06	Click the location in the document to which you want to move
List box, scroll	WIN 1.26	Click the list arrow for the list box to display the list of options; click the scroll down or up arrow; or drag the scroll box
Menu option, select	WIN 1.23	Click the option on the menu; for submenus, point to an option on the menu
My Computer, open	WIN 2.12	Double-click the My Computer icon on the desktop
Program, close	WIN 1.12	Click ☒
Program, close inactive	WIN 1.15	Right-click the program button on the taskbar, click Close
Program, start	WIN 1.11	*See* Reference Window: Starting a Program
Program, switch to another	WIN 1.14	Click the program button on the taskbar
ScreenTips, view	WIN 1.05	Position pointer over an item
Start menu, open	WIN 1.06	Click **start**
Text, select	WIN 2.06	Drag the pointer over the text
Toolbar button, select	WIN 1.25	Click the toolbar button
Toolbars, control display	WIN 2.20	Click View, point to Toolbars, select the toolbar options you want
Window, close	WIN 1.12	Click ☒
Window, maximize	WIN 1.20	Click ☐
Window, minimize	WIN 1.20	Click ▭
Window, move	WIN 1.21	Drag the title bar
Window, resize	WIN 1.21	Drag
Window, restore	WIN 1.21	Click ▣
Windows XP, shut down	WIN 1.15	Click **start**, click Turn Off Computer, click the Turn Off button
Windows XP, start	WIN 1.02	Turn on the computer

Windows XP Level I File Finder

Location in Tutorial	Name and Location of Data File	Student Saves File As...	Student Creates New File
Tutorial 1	No Data Files needed		
Tutorial 2			
Session 2.1			Practice Text.txt
Session 2.2 *Note*: Students copy the contents of Disk 1 onto Disk 2 in this session.	Agenda.rtf Beck.asx Holiday.bmp Iceberg.jpg Logo.bmp New Logo.bmp Proposal.rtf Resume.rtf Salinas Family.eml Stationery.bmp Vinca.jpg Practice Text.txt *(saved from Session 2.1)*		
Review Assignments and Projects *Note*: Students continue to use the Data Disks they used in the Tutorial. For certain Assignments, they need a third blank disk.	Resume.rtf	Woods Resume.rtf	Letter.rtf Song.rtf Poem.rtf